MAKE YOUR OWN

MAKE YOUR OWN

120+ MINIMALLY PROCESSED, OIL-FREE, WHEAT-FREE, SUGAR-FREE, PLANT-BASED RECIPES

Javant Benton

New York Boston

This book is not intended as a substitute for medical advice of physicians. The reader should regularly consult a physician in all matters relating to his or her health, and particularly in respect of any symptoms that may require diagnosis or medical attention.

Interior photographs (author) © Venu Gopal Photography; (food) © Sam Adler Photography

Cover design by Terri Sirma.
Cover photograph (author) © Venu Gopal Photography; (food) © Sam Adler Photography
Cover copyright © 2026 by Hachette Book Group, Inc.

Balance
Hachette Book Group
1290 Avenue of the Americas
New York, NY 10104
GCP-Balance.com
@GCPBalance

First Edition: March 2026

Balance is an imprint of Grand Central Publishing. The Balance name and logo are registered trademarks of Hachette Book Group, Inc.

Print book interior design by Toni Tajima

Library of Congress Control Number: 2025028895

ISBNs: 978-0-306-83669-5 (paper over board), 978-0-306-83670-1 (ebook)

Printed in China

TLF

10 9 8 7 6 5 4 3 2

This book is dedicated to my family members
who have passed away too soon, and to all those who
have faced health challenges—past and present—
may you be empowered to care for yourselves while
inspiring the future generations to prioritize their
health and well-being.

Contents

BREAKFAST

HIGH-PROTEIN SNACKS

DRINKS

SANDWICHES AND WRAPS

SALADS, BOWLS, AND SOUPS

MAIN DISHES

DESSERTS

Foreword

This book has the potential to save millions of lives.

Our health future is shaped by our eating habits—you can control your health destiny with excellent nutrition. And one great chef can help you transform your health more than thousands of doctors prescribing medications. Javant Benton is that one chef: He has made healthy eating taste so good, everyone should be able to do it.

There is an overwhelming amount of evidence in the scientific literature from hundreds of studies that higher consumption of vegetables decreases the risk of both heart disease and cancer. Green vegetables, mushrooms, and onions have shown remarkable ability to slow aging, lower blood pressure, lower cholesterol, and prevent cancer. Greens, beans, onions, mushrooms, berries, and seeds are the six most evidence-based, health-promoting, anticancer foods. And the recipes in this cookbook are full of these G-BOMBS. In my Nutritarian diet I suggest including these foods almost every day. This eating style supplies the vital micronutrients and phytochemicals that help prevent inflammation and support normal immune function, and protects us against harm from dangerous infections.

This way of eating is the pinnacle of longevity diets. It emphasizes whole plant foods: greens, vegetables, fruits, seeds, and nuts. It limits meat, dairy, and other animal products and avoids oil, concentrated sweeteners, white flour products, processed foods, and excess sodium. Why put something in your mouth that is self-destructive to your own health future?

There's well-established, scientific evidence that most chronic diseases can be reversed by eating this way. This is a message of hope, touted by thousands of nutritional scientists and physicians. Unfortunately, our taste buds have been hijacked by too many sweeteners, salt, and hyperpalatable processed foods and fast foods. The recipes found in *Make Your Own* offer a delicious course correction: They will have you enjoying healthy, wholesome meals more and more as you go. You can lose your food addiction to self-destructive foods. You won't just learn fantastic recipes, but your tastes will also change so you actually prefer healthier foods.

Javant's cooking style makes it easy to eat this way; you can keep it simple or you can make it gourmet. He mixes simplicity with some incredible delicious gourmet options—and there are hundreds of those options right here. You do not have to forgo the pleasure of eating to have great health.

This way of eating can really impact the health of our country. This diet makes it easy to lose weight and keep it off—without counting calories. The scientific evidence is clear: You can be leaner, stronger, and live longer without cardiovascular disease and cancer in your future—but you must make major changes. I know with this fantastic cookbook, you can do it.

Joel Fuhrman, MD
7 times *New York Times* bestselling author
Board-Certified Family Physician
President, Nutritional Research Foundation
Visit him at DrFuhrman.com

INTRODUCTION

My grandmother's cooking was the stuff of family legend. Her meals embodied everything we associate with comfort food: rich, savory, and sweet. I grew up on her pancakes, pecan pie, fried chicken, and other Southern classics like mac and cheese, sweet potato pie, and corn bread. These meals were home to me and the rest of my family. But while they symbolized comfort, I now know they weren't made with the healthiest ingredients.

Javant's grandmother with Javant and his cousin (top); Javant's grandmother (bottom)

As a child, I watched my grandmother, aunts, uncles, and other loved ones rely on medications for diabetes, high blood pressure, and other all-too-common illnesses. I was conditioned to believe that these health issues were an inevitable part of life, something that affected everyone by the time they hit their thirties or forties. I grew up thinking that one day I too would find myself taking medications, as if it were unavoidable. And that was, indeed, almost my path!

Cooking wasn't something I ever considered a passion or even a hobby. My journey into healthier cooking began out of necessity. For the first thirty-five years of my life, I enjoyed those traditional comfort foods without much thought, until reality hit. I found myself eighty-five pounds overweight, prediabetic,

Javant before (top);
Javant after (bottom)

and prehypertensive. Doctors began running tests to explore what could be a serious underlying health issue.

Admittedly, I was scared, but I've never been one to embrace feelings of helplessness. I believe knowledge is power, so I empowered myself by researching and studying the work of many prominent doctors in the health field. Gradually, I learned which foods are considered disease promoting and which are health promoting. Over time, I discovered how to reduce, eliminate, and incorporate certain foods to create healthier versions of the dishes I loved.

This newfound knowledge transformed the way I approached food and cooking. It wasn't just about survival; it became a way to reclaim my health, break free from the conditioning I grew up with, and rediscover the joy of nourishing myself in ways that felt good for my body, mind, and soul. Today, I still enjoy my favorite nostalgic foods but with a twist. I've re-created them using minimally processed ingredients, completely free of animal products, oil, wheat, and refined sugar.

MAKING MY OWN

Currently, some statistics indicate that nearly 50 percent of Americans have diabetes or prediabetes, whether they know it or not.[1] Furthermore, approximately 74 percent of Americans are overweight or obese,[2] which puts them at a significantly higher risk for chronic diseases like diabetes, as well as high blood pressure, cardiovascular disease, stroke, and even cancer.

We have been conditioned to rely on ultraprocessed and refined foods in the name of convenience, with little or no thought given to the long-term effects of these foods. Unfortunately, as eating a standard American diet has become the norm, so too have the ailments it produces. Often people who adopt a vegan diet also rely on heavily processed products. Many meat and dairy replacements are junk foods filled with additives, thickeners, saturated fats, and excessive amounts of sodium, all of which can negatively affect health. However, learning to prepare meals with a healthy vegan (HV) approach eliminates these types of products by empowering you to make your own healthier versions of plant-based meats, cheeses, and other dairy replacements.

Research has consistently shown that reducing or eliminating processed foods, animal products, oils, refined wheat, and refined sugars from our diets can improve and, in some cases, reverse some of our most common diseases. Renowned health experts, such as Dr. Joel Fuhrman, Dr. Michael Greger, and

---

1 CDC, "National Diabetes Statistics Report," May 15, 2024, https://www.cdc.gov/diabetes/php/data-research/index.html.

2 Linda Searing, "About 74 Percent of Adults in the U.S. Are Overweight, According to the CDC," *Washington Post*, December 18, 2020, https://www.washingtonpost.com/health/most-american-adults-are-overweight/2020/12/18/faefa834-408d-11eb-9453-fc36ba051781_story.html.

Dr. T. Colin Campbell, have extensively documented and share evidence-based strategies for achieving better health through dietary changes.[3]

Adopting a diet centered around whole, minimally processed plant foods is not only about avoiding disease; it's about thriving and feeling your best every day. Back when I was unhealthy and needed to make a change to eat healthier foods, I had no idea how to start. The idea of preparing foods without the use of oil, refined sugar, and wheat that would also taste great seemed challenging and intimidating. However, through lots of reading, trial and error, and, eventually, successes, I slowly gained momentum and learned to create delicious HV versions of all my childhood and adult favorites. Eating my newly created HV dishes resulted in weight loss and reversed my prediabetes and hypertension. I was so blown away with the healing power of delicious-tasting healthy food that I was inspired to somehow share this approach with others. It was my passion to share the power of making your own that led me to social media and allowed me to, eventually, amass over a million followers who resonated with the healthy vegan, Make Your Own approach. The HV message is simple: With the want-to and the know-how, you can create delicious, nutritious meals that nourish your body and improve your overall well-being. My hope is that this book will empower you to do exactly that.

---

3 Here are just a few resources: Center for Nutrition Studies, "Living a Whole Food, Plant-Based Life," https://nutritionstudies.org/whole-food-plant-based-diet-guide/; Michael Greger, "What Is the Healthiest Diet?," NutritionFacts.org, https://nutritionfacts.org/; and Joel Fuhrman, "Beginner's Guide to the Nutritarian Diet," Dr. Fuhrman (blog), https://www.drfuhrman.com/blog/210/beginners-guide?srsltid=AfmBOorDWbJiHnTgP1QMgFVKD0WJr2GseOsE4iYFQAVXlelxL9CXpH-l.

Check out these books: Joel Fuhrman, *Eat for Life* (New York: HarperOne, 2020); Michael Greger, *How Not to Die* (New York: Flatiron Books, 2015); and T. Colin Campbell and Howard Jacobson, *Whole* (Dallas, TX: BenBella Books, 2014).

THE FOUNDATIONS

WHOLE FOOD FATS

Not all oils are created equal, and some are definitely healthier options than others. Extra-virgin olive oil and avocado oil are two of the better choices. However, there are some aspects to all oils (including extra-virgin olive oil and avocado oil) that cause me to opt for healthier alternatives, namely nuts, seeds, and avocados. Here is why:

- **Oil** is a refined product consisting of 100 percent fat with no fiber and few essential nutrients. A single tablespoon has 120 calories, and a quarter cup contains 480 calories, so it doesn't take much to overconsume it, which promotes weight gain. It's true that olive oil contains some beneficial monounsaturated fats and polyphenols with antioxidant and anti-inflammatory properties, but it pales in comparison to the nutrient density of whole foods like nuts, seeds, and avocados.
- **Extracted oils,** including olive oil, are absorbed quickly by the body, leading to rapid fat storage rather than utilization for energy. Comparatively, the calories and fat from nuts and seeds are absorbed more slowly, providing sustained energy without overly contributing to weight gain.
- **Nuts** are more nutrient dense overall, providing fiber, protein, and a broader array of vitamins and minerals. This is why I choose to use nuts and seeds to replace oil in many of my recipes. And, trust me, once you taste the results, you won't miss oil at all!

WHOLE UNREFINED GRAINS

When wheat is refined, it's stripped of its bran and germ. These two parts contain nearly all the vitamins, minerals, antioxidants, and fiber. What's left is mostly starch and a little protein. The absence of fiber in refined wheat results in it getting digested quickly, leading to spikes in blood sugar and insulin. Over time, these spikes can increase the risk of conditions like prediabetes and eventually type 2 diabetes.

If you think about the types of foods made from refined wheat, it's a who's who of unhealthy foods. Foods like crackers, pastries, cookies, donuts, cakes, bagels, bread, pizza, and more. Along with refined wheat, these foods are often loaded with sugar, unhealthy fats, and preservatives—ingredients that promote disease, not health.

Whole, unrefined grains like millet and quinoa, a pseudo-grain, contain antioxidants and other nutrients that help nourish our bodies. When wheat is refined, these beneficial compounds are lost.

DATES, THE SUPERIOR SWEETENER

When it comes to the detrimental effects of refined sugar, the list is so long I could write another book discussing it. However, here are a few reasons I don't use any refined sugar in my recipes. Refined sugar gets absorbed almost instantly into the bloodstream, causing rapid blood sugar spikes and subsequent crashes. Over time, this can lead to insulin resistance and eventually type 2 diabetes. Foods high in refined sugar typically are high in calories and lack micronutrients, which can result in overeating and excess fat on the body. My preferred replacement for sugar is dates. Dates have a relatively low glycemic index, which means they won't raise your blood sugar as high as most other sweeteners. Dates are also a whole food that contains antioxidants, minerals, vitamins, and fiber, which help to slow their digestion. Dates are generally considered a healthy sweetener for diabetics, if not overconsumed.

THE POWER OF SELF-LOVE IN TRANSFORMING THE WAY YOU EAT

One thing I have learned through personal experience and observation is that most people struggle when attempting to transition to a healthier diet. This is particularly true if we allow the need for social approval or peer pressure to influence our eating and lifestyle habits. Once you are conditioned into negative eating patterns, transitioning to healthier food choices may no longer be strictly a matter of willpower or discipline; it could be about learning to value yourself beyond external validation. When we consistently seek outside validation from our partners, friends, and family, needing their approval can become just as addictive as eating junk food.

When our first and primary focus is self-care, self-love, and self-esteem, we are much more likely to make healthy food choices regardless of how we are judged by those around us. When we consistently nourish ourselves with a healthy diet, it not only makes us feel better physically but also makes us feel better mentally and emotionally. It's really empowering knowing that we have our own best interests at heart and that we are taking care of ourselves without the need to have everyone's approval to be happy and content.

Making healthy diet and lifestyle changes and sticking with them can seem difficult at first. This is particularly true in societies where most people choose to be reactive rather than proactive regarding their health. However, the sense of accomplishment, joy, and health gained from consistently eating nutritious foods will far outweigh any negative elements of your journey to health. You must be determined to put you and your health first! This mindset and way of life will be the catalyst that puts you on a path to long-term health and happiness powered by an authentic self-love that comes from within, instead of the validation of others.

If you are hurting or afraid because your health is not where you want it to be, or if you are struggling with emotional eating, not sure how to go about losing weight, received a scary diagnosis, or just want to improve how you feel, remember the transition starts within. Develop the want-to, then seek the know-how. Having the desire and acquiring the knowledge to transition to a healthier lifestyle are not just steps you must take to get started; they are the steps that will lead you all the way to your ultimate goal: becoming the healthiest you that you can be. It all starts with self-worth and self-love, and only you can give you that!

I know it's easy for me to say all this, but I also know everyone is on their own journey and has their own struggles. It can be hard to make change, so here are a few tips to help you get started.

HOW TO USE THIS BOOK

We are in a time when convenience meals are everywhere. *Make Your Own* is about taking back control while simplifying the process of putting together a meal that's nourishing, satisfying, and free of the usual not-so-great ingredients. I want this book to empower you to create simple, wholesome meals that still fit into a busy lifestyle, without feeling overwhelmed or resorting to ultraprocessed shortcuts. For the most part, these recipes require pretty basic ingredients—many of which you may already have on hand. Before we get to the recipes, I will be sharing a list of key ingredients and kitchen tools. Here are some additional things to consider:

- **Ingredients.** Some of the ingredients below may be new to you and may require some additional sourcing; this is where ordering online or buying locally in bulk can be a huge help.
- **Swaps.** My goal is for these recipes to be flexible to fit your taste preferences and your pantry. When a recipe calls for nut butter or plant milk, you should feel free to use your favorite kind. See recipe notes for any specifics on ingredient swaps.
- **Master the Basics.** Start with exploring the MYO Staples section of this book. These recipes are the perfect foundation for creating healthier versions of the foods you love. Check out the MYO Meals Matrix (page 10) for ideas on how to start redesigning your meals, HV-style!

- **Easy Meal Prep.** I've started the recipe section with MYO Staples, and I suggest planning and preparing Staple recipes weekly to have on hand for easy meal prep—with healthy staples at your fingertips, you are setting yourself up to easily create nutrient-dense, delicious meals. Make a batch of my HV Veggie Ground (page 30) for anytime burgers or no-meatballs; keep extra Jalapeño Lime Sauce (page 60) on hand for any time you want to add a kick to soup, sandwiches, or salads. And if you love mayo, be sure to keep my MaYO (page 40) on hand. Most of the recipes lend well to doubling or even tripling.
- **Quick and Easy.** I've listed difficulty ratings for each recipe; you'll find most of them are Easy. For the ones noted as a bit more difficult, that is mostly due to extra time or processes like rolling out dough. Even if you are new to cooking, you should be able to make these recipes successfully.
- **Make What You Love, and You'll Love What You Make!** Many people find it helpful to make HV versions of the foods they are familiar with and enjoy eating. Are burgers, pasta, and cookies your favorites? Then check out my Better Bacon Cheeseburger (page 154), Veggie Sausage Lasagna (page 198), or my Chewy Chocolate Chip Cookies (page 235).
- **Learn and Adapt.** Preparing food HV-style will allow you to learn new methods around cooking that may not be intuitive to some. Take notice of recurring cooking methods and ingredients used in my recipes, and you'll be able to healthy veganize any meal!

MYO Meals Matrix

STAPLE	RECIPE	OTHER WAYS TO USE IT!
HV Veggie Ground	No-Meatball Gyro (page 149) MYO Burrito (page 150) The Better Bacon Cheeseburger (page 154) Greek-Style Burger (page 157) Nacho Salad Bowl (page 164) Sweet Potato Chili Cheese Fries (page 187) Burger and Ranch Pizza (page 205) Teriyaki No-Meatballs (page 200) No-Meatloaf (page 203) Sweet Potato Shepherd's Pie (page 207) Jamaican Patties (page 221)	Tacos Chili Quesadillas Pasta sauce Cabbage rolls Stuffed peppers
Veggie Sausage Ground	Breakfast Sausage Patties (page 86) Veggie Sausage Lasagna (page 198)	Tacos Wraps Quesadillas Pasta sauce Stuffed peppers
Chick'n-Style Mushrooms	No-Chick'n Caesar Wrap (page 138) No-Chick'n Enchilada Casserole (page 211)	Tacos Fajitas Quesadillas Salads and bowls
Easy Cheese Sauce	MYO Burrito (page 150) The Better Bacon Cheeseburger (page 154) Portobello Fajitas (page 184) Sweet Potato Chili Cheese Fries (page 187) Sweet Potato Shepherd's Pie (page 207) No-Chick'n Enchilada Casserole (page 211) Veggie Sausage Lasagna (page 198)	Sandwiches Bowls Pasta Tacos
MaYO	Pulled BBQ Jackfruit Sandwich (page 142) Chickpea No-Tuna Salad Sandwich (page 146) HV BLT (page 145) No-Crab Cakes (page 190) Sushi Salad Bowl (page 167)	Sandwiches and wraps Dips Sauces Potato salad Vegan egg salad Vegan chick'n salad

STAPLE	RECIPE	OTHER WAYS TO USE IT!
Classic Sour Cream	20-Minute Chickpea Tacos (page 153) Three-Bean Chili (page 189)	Sandwiches Dips Sauces Dressings
Simple Tomato Sauce	Veggie Sausage Lasagna (page 198) Burger and Ranch Pizza (page 205)	Pasta Stuffed peppers Cabbage rolls Stuffed zucchini
Date Paste	High-Protein Loaf Bread (page 48) Wheat-Free Cinnamon Raisin Bread (page 77) Gluten-Free Millet Burger Buns (page 52) Spicy Mango Buffalo Sauce (page 57) Teriyaki Sauce (page 60) Mixed Berry Breakfast Bars (page 78) Mango-Coconut Chia Pudding (page 93) Strawberry Cheesecake Baked Oats (page 94) Carrot Cake Overnight Oats (page 98) Chocolate-Strawberry Overnight Oats (page 98) Lemon-Blueberry Breakfast Cookies (page 103) Strawberry–Chocolate Chip Breakfast Cookies (page 104) Golden Breakfast Cookies (page 105) Carrot Cake Breakfast Cookies (page 106) Pulled BBQ Jackfruit Sandwich (page 142) Chunky Vegetable Tomato Soup (page 175) No-Meatloaf (page 203) Simple Chocolate Turtles (page 229) Peanut Butter Cups (page 226) Strawberry-Fig Cookies (page 231) Chewy Chocolate Chip Cookies (page 235) Sesame Date Cookies (page 236) Cherry Pistachio Cookies (page 239) Brownie Cookies (page 244) Apple Crumb Pie (page 261)	Top pancakes Use it as a caramel-style dip for fruits Pair it with nut or seed butter of choice for toast or bagel Sweeten drinks, smoothies, sauces

MYO Meals Matrix, *continued*

STAPLE	RECIPE	OTHER WAYS TO USE IT!
Wheat-Free Breadcrumbs	No-Crab Cakes (page 190) Sticky Teriyaki Cauliflower Wings (page 180) Mango Buffalo Mushroom Wings (page 183) Veggie Sausage Lasagna (page 198)	Topping for salads and pastas Breading vegetables and mushrooms Binding burgers and vegetable patties
Extra-Crunchy Wheat-Free Breadcrumbs	No-Crab Cakes (page 190) Sticky Teriyaki Cauliflower Wings (page 180) Mango Buffalo Mushroom Wings (page 183) Veggie Sausage Lasagna (page 198)	Topping for salads and pastas Breading vegetables and mushrooms Binding burgers and vegetable patties
High-Protein Loaf Bread	HV BLT (page 145) Chickpea No-Tuna Salad Sandwich (page 146)	Avocado toast Sandwiches No Egg, Soy-Free Breakfast Scramble (page 89) Accompany soups and stews
Soft Almond Flatbread	No-Chick'n Caesar Wrap (page 138) Island-Style Jerk Pulled Mushroom Wrap (page 141) No-Meatball Gyro (page 149) MYO Burrito (page 150) Portobello Fajitas (page 184)	Tacos Quesadillas Wraps
Gluten-Free Millet Burger Buns	HV BLT (page 145) Chickpea No-Tuna Salad Sandwich (page 146) The Better Bacon Cheeseburger (page 154) Greek-Style Burger (page 157)	Burgers Sandwiches

STOCKING YOUR MYO KITCHEN

INGREDIENTS

Below is a list of ingredients that I frequently use in these recipes. These ingredients can be found in conventional grocery stores, health-food stores, and online. Of course, variety and availability will vary depending on your specific location.

Agar Agar Powder. A plant-based gelling agent derived from red seaweed, agar agar serves as a fantastic vegan alternative to gelatin. I use it to set my Mango-Chocolate Cheesecake and Key Lime Cheesecake recipes (see pages 270, 273). The recipes in this book call for agar agar powder rather than flakes. If you use the latter, the amounts will differ. You can purchase agar agar at some health-food stores, Asian markets, and online.

Almond Flour. Made simply from finely ground almonds, almond flour is one of my favorite ingredients for creating wheat-free cakes and cookies. Its naturally sweet, nutty flavor enhances recipes, and when paired with oat flour, it creates a nice, soft texture. Once a specialty item, almond flour has become widely available and can now be found in most major grocery stores.

Apple Cider Vinegar. Apple cider vinegar adds a tangy, sour flavor that I find closely resembles the taste of fermented dairy products like sour cream. I love incorporating it into sauces, dressings, and my mayo for its unique depth of flavor. Additionally, it plays a key role in my baking recipes as a leavening agent. When combined with baking soda or baking powder, it helps create a lighter, fluffier texture in breads and cakes.

If you're avoiding apple cider vinegar, lemon juice is a great alternative. Keep in mind, however, that its slightly lower acidity may result in a minor difference in leavening, so you might notice a subtle variation in texture.

Arrowroot Powder. A starch derived from the rootstock of the *Maranta arundinacea* plant, arrowroot powder is a versatile ingredient. It's ideal for adding lightness to recipes, as well as for thickening and binding. You can find it at most health-food stores or online.

Baking Powder and Baking Soda. Baking soda, also known as sodium bicarbonate, is a naturally occurring mineral with two primary sources in the United States, trona and nahcolite. My preference is nahcolite-sourced baking soda, which is mined in Colorado and undergoes minimal processing compared to trona-based alternatives.

One important note: Baking soda is high in sodium, so it may not be ideal for those aiming to reduce or eliminate sodium intake. While potassium bicarbonate serves as a sodium-free substitute, it is challenging to source naturally.

In baking, baking soda plays a crucial role as a leavening agent. When combined with an acid, it produces carbon dioxide, creating a lighter, airier texture in doughs and batters. Baking powder, another common leavening agent, serves a similar purpose but is a premixed combination of sodium bicarbonate, an acidic compound (often containing aluminum), and a starch, such as cornstarch. For those concerned about potentially less healthy ingredients in store-bought baking powder, making your own is a simple and healthier alternative.

HOMEMADE BAKING POWDER RECIPE

- 2 parts cream of tartar (a natural by-product of winemaking)
- 1 part baking soda
- 1 part arrowroot powder

Combine all the ingredients until well mixed; store in an airtight jar or container.

When I cook for myself, I often minimize or omit leavening agents, as I don't mind sacrificing the lighter texture they provide. However, I do include them in recipes meant for others, as they significantly improve the overall texture and quality of baked goods.

Beans and Legumes. Beans and legumes are a staple in my diet, and I enjoy them every single day. They are a good source of health-promoting fiber, resistant starch, protein, folate, and iron and provide a wide array of health benefits, many of which I highlight in the recipes featured in this book. In fact, the renowned "Food Habits in Later Life" study, which looked at the effect of nine different food groups on longevity, showed that "higher legume intake is the most protective dietary predictor of survival amongst the elderly."[4] They are not only incredibly nutritious but also one of the most budget-friendly options available. While you can find cooked beans conveniently packaged in cans, jars, or tetra packs, I personally prefer buying

4 Irene Darmadi-Blackberry et al., "Legumes: The Most Important Dietary Predictor of Survival in Older People of Different Ethnicities," *Asia-Pacific Journal* 13, no. 2 (2004): 217–220.

them dry and cooking them at home for optimal freshness. These recipes primarily use chickpeas, cannellini, and black beans.

Cashews (raw). When it comes to achieving a smooth, creamy texture, raw cashews are my go-to. Their neutral flavor allows them to create a rich base without overpowering or altering the dish's taste. For the best results, soak your raw cashews for at least four hours and blend them with a high-speed blender to achieve the smoothest, creamiest consistency.

Chia Seeds. Chia seeds come in two varieties: black and white. Both varieties offer similar benefits, but I prefer the white ones, as they don't alter the color of the dishes they are used in. Chia seeds have a unique ability to thicken while maintaining a neutral flavor, making them ideal for creating quick and delicious puddings (page 93). They're also a good source of plant protein and omega-3 fatty acids, making them a perfect addition to my plant-based protein shakes (pages 116–120). Use ground chia seeds to substitute for ground flaxseed in many recipes featured in this book. For optimal health benefits, remember to grind or soak them before use. You can find them in most grocery stores these days, as well as online.

Chickpea Flour. Chickpea flour is made from ground chickpeas and is generally a great choice of flour. In this book, I use it specifically as a binder for recipes like burgers (page 154) and veggie meatballs (page 200). When used sparingly, its flavor, often considered an acquired taste, is subtle and blends seamlessly into the dish. It's best used in savory dishes, as its texture and distinct flavor don't work very well in baked goods. You can find it in natural grocery stores, specialty grocery stores (Indian or Middle Eastern), and online.

Chocolate Chips. When selecting chocolate, I prefer date-sweetened or unsweetened chocolate chips. If your taste buds aren't yet accustomed to reduced sugar, unsweetened chocolate might taste too bitter for you. In that case, date-sweetened chocolate chips are a great alternative. A few brands offer date-sweetened options, which are available at larger health-food stores or online.

Cocoa and Cacao Powder. Cacao and cocoa powder can be used interchangeably in the recipes featured in this book. Cacao, derived from raw, unprocessed cacao beans, is more nutritionally dense, offering a richer array of nutrients. While cocoa is less nutrient-dense due to the roasting process, it remains a healthy option. You can get both of these at most conventional grocery stores, health-food stores, and online.

Coconut Aminos. An excellent soy-free alternative to soy sauce and tamari, coconut aminos are made from the nectar of coconut palm flower buds. They bring a salty yet slightly sweet flavor to dishes, with the benefit of significantly lower sodium. However, not all coconut aminos are created equal: Some can be overly watery with muted flavors while others offer a richer, more robust taste and a syrupy consistency. To ensure the best results, choose a high-quality brand that balances salty and sweet flavors. I suggest experimenting with different brands to discover your favorite.

I incorporate coconut aminos into a wide range of dishes, not just as a flavor enhancer, but also as a versatile substitute for oil. Their texture helps seasonings adhere evenly to ingredients, which creates an added depth of flavor to dishes.

Coconut aminos are readily available in the ethnic section at most grocery stores, health-food stores, and online.

Coconut Milk. Coconut milk is an ingredient I use sparingly due to its high saturated fat content. However, you'll see it used in a few recipes throughout this book, often as a nut-free alternative to cashew cream. Whenever possible, I've included substitutions for coconut milk to accommodate different preferences or dietary needs.

Dates. Dates are a delicious and nutritious way to naturally sweeten foods and desserts. Unlike refined sugar, dates are a whole food, meaning they retain all their fiber and nutrients. The fiber in dates helps slow the absorption of sugar into the bloodstream, reducing the risk of blood sugar spikes.

For this reason, all the recipes in this book are sweetened exclusively with date-based sweeteners, primarily whole dates and date paste (see page 43). Date paste is made by blending whole dates with water to create a smooth, creamy consistency. While you can sometimes find date paste in ethnic food stores, the consistency can vary significantly. To ensure the best results in these recipes, I recommend using my homemade date paste recipe for consistency and flavor.

The two most common date varieties found in the United States and Canada are Deglet Noor and Medjool dates. Deglet Noor dates are smaller and drier compared to the larger, softer Medjool dates. Personally, I prefer Medjool dates because their softness makes them easier to blend into a smooth and creamy paste or sauces and dressings. You can find dates at most conventional and health-food stores, as well as online.

Date Sugar. Date sugar is made by grinding whole, dehydrated dates into a fine powder. Unlike refined sugars, it retains all the fiber from the fruit, making it a much healthier alternative.

However, date sugar behaves differently when used in recipes. It does not dissolve like other sugars when heated, so it's not always a direct substitute for traditional sugars or liquid sweeteners. In this book, I've included date sugar in two recipes, Wheat-Free Cinnamon Raisin Bread (page 77) and Quinoa Breakfast Bagels (page 72) because it provides the perfect natural sweetness for these baked goods. You can get date sugar at most health-food stores and online.

Date Syrup. Date syrup is a cooked, concentrated form of date paste, with a consistency and flavor similar to molasses. Its concentrated nature makes it sweeter than date paste, so you need less to achieve the desired level of sweetness. While it's arguably one of the healthiest liquid sweeteners, it is a more processed option, as some of the natural fiber is removed during production. For this reason, I reserve its use for only a handful of recipes. You can find it at most health-food stores and online.

Flaxseed. Flaxseed is a great source of plant-based omega-3 fatty acids, protein, and numerous health-promoting compounds known to offer protective benefits against breast cancer and other forms of cancer. Throughout this book, you'll find ground flaxseed incorporated into protein shakes, protein bars, desserts, and more. I prefer the golden flaxseed variety because it has a milder flavor while still providing similar benefits. Notably, ground flaxseed serves as an excellent egg substitute in many plant-based baked goods, making it a versatile and nutritious ingredient. Flaxseed is readily available in both health-food stores and conventional grocery stores as well as online.

Hearts of Palm. Hearts of palm have a soft, slightly fibrous texture and a mild, neutral flavor, making them a versatile addition to dishes like my No-Crab Cakes (page 190). Typically found in cans or occasionally in jars, they are widely available at most health-food stores and can also be conveniently purchased online. However, it's worth noting that canned and jarred hearts of palm often contain significant amounts of sodium. If you're watching your sodium intake, I recommend draining and soaking them overnight to reduce the salt content before incorporating them into your recipes.

Hemp Hearts. Hemp hearts, also referred to as hemp seeds, are an excellent source of plant-based protein and omega-3 fatty acids. I enjoy adding them to my protein shakes (pages 116–120) as a wholesome and natural protein boost. They also work beautifully as a creamy addition when combined with white beans in my nut-free alternative to cashew-based sauces. You may also see hemp hearts used in combination with cashews to improve the omega profile of some recipes. Versatile and nutrient-rich, hemp hearts are easy to find at health-food stores and online.

Jackfruit. Jackfruit is a large tropical fruit, prized for its ability to mimic the texture of some meat dishes. For the recipes in this book, you'll be using young jackfruit, the unripe fruit harvested before it develops its natural sweetness. Its soft, fibrous texture and mild flavor make it an excellent meat substitute. I particularly love using it in recipes like Pulled BBQ Jackfruit Sandwich (page 142), where it absorbs the flavors of the seasonings and sauces it's paired with.

Young jackfruit is typically sold in cans or jars, which means it often contains a significant amount of sodium. To reduce both the sodium content and its briny taste, rinse the jackfruit thoroughly and boil it for ten minutes before incorporating it into your dishes. You can find canned jackfruit at some conventional grocery stores, most health-food stores, Trader Joe's, and online.

Millet. Pearl millet, my favorite grain for replacing rice, offers a nutty flavor and a slightly firm texture when cooked. It pairs wonderfully with a variety of dishes, making it a versatile rice alternative. Rich in vitamins and minerals and low on the glycemic index, pearl millet is a nutritious choice. Pearl millet can be found in health-food stores and online.

Millet Flour. Made simply by grinding pearl millet, millet flour is one of my favorite alternatives for creating a wheat-free loaf bread. It has a subtly earthy flavor and a lighter texture compared to whole wheat, making it a good choice for baking. You can find millet flour at many health-food stores and online, or even make your own by grinding whole pearl millet in a high-speed blender or seed grinder.

Miso Paste. A traditional Japanese seasoning known for its rich, savory taste, miso paste is a prime example of umami flavor. Made by fermenting soybeans with salt and koji (a culture typically grown on rice or barley), miso has a complex profile that is salty, slightly sweet, and fermented. While it's a staple in many Japanese-inspired dishes, I have found that miso paste also serves as a good substitute for nutritional yeast and have added it as a suggested substitute in my recipes when appropriate.

There are light and dark varieties of miso, with the dark typically indicating a longer fermentation time. I personally use dark miso, but light will work as well. You can find it at some grocery stores, as well as Asian markets.

For those avoiding soy, there are now miso options made from chickpeas. If you're also steering clear of rice, as I do, look for chickpea miso made with barley koji. This unique product is available online.

Mushrooms. In this book, I highlight a variety of mushrooms, each offering unique health benefits. Mushrooms are an exceptional ingredient, not only for their nutritional value but also for their ability to mimic the texture traditionally associated with meat. With the right seasonings and cooking technique, they will satisfy both vegans and meat eaters alike, making them a versatile addition to many dishes.

Common varieties like white button and portobello mushrooms are widely available in most grocery stores. Shiitake mushrooms are often found in health-food stores and Asian markets. For more exotic varieties, such as lion's mane and oyster mushrooms, availability can vary depending on your location, but they can often be found at health-food stores, Asian markets, or local farmers' markets.

If sourcing them proves difficult, growing your own is a fantastic alternative. Home-growing kits for lion's mane and oyster mushrooms are becoming increasingly accessible, allowing you to enjoy fresh, flavorful mushrooms grown right in your home.

Nut and/or Seed Butters. When selecting nut or seed butters, I prefer brands that are raw and free from added sugar, salt, or oil. For most recipes, I typically use almond or cashew butter. If a nut-free option is needed, tahini (sesame seed butter) is my go-to choice. Feel free to use your favorite nut or seed butter in any of the recipes throughout this book.

Nutritional Yeast. A deactivated yeast, nutritional yeast is a popular ingredient in vegan cooking that is used for its cheesy, umami flavor. When selecting a brand, I recommend using certified organic and nonfortified varieties to minimize the potential for genetically modified ingredients and synthetic vitamins. You can find it in some conventional grocery stores, health-food stores, and online.

If you're avoiding nutritional yeast, miso paste serves as an excellent alternative, providing a similar depth of flavor.

Plant Milk. Plant milk refers to nondairy alternatives made from plants, such as almond, oat, cashew, or, my personal favorite, walnut milk. While many of these options can work, when purchasing plant milks, it's important to note that many plant milks are loaded with synthetic vitamins, oils, and thickeners. Fortunately, there are brands available that use only two or three simple ingredients—or you can skip the store-bought versions altogether by making your own at home.

HOMEMADE WALNUT MILK

- 1 cup walnuts, soaked for 6–8 hours
- 3 cups filtered water (use more or less for a thicker or thinner consistency)
- Dates and vanilla extract to taste (optional)

1. Drain and rinse the walnuts. Put them in a high-speed blender with the water and, if using, the dates and vanilla extract. Blend until smooth.

2. Using a nut milk bag or colander lined with cheesecloth, strain the milk until only the pulp remains. This will require some manual squeezing.

3. Store the milk in the fridge for up to 4 days.

Zero waste: Store the pulp in the freezer and add it to smoothies or salads.

Protein Powder. This book includes four protein bar recipes (pages 110–115) that use unflavored, unsweetened protein powder. When selecting a high-quality protein powder, I recommend choosing one that is certified organic and made exclusively with plant-based protein ingredients. Be sure to avoid powders with artificial additives, sweeteners, or preservatives for the best results and a cleaner ingredient profile.

Quinoa. With its nutty flavor, quinoa is a nutrient-dense alternative to rice that pairs beautifully with most dishes. While technically a seed and not a grain, quinoa stands out as a great source of plant protein. It's widely available in health-food stores, conventional grocery stores, and online. Quinoa comes in three varieties: white, red, and black, all offering similar nutritional benefits. Personally, I prefer the red and black varieties for their slightly chewier texture and resilience, they're less likely to turn mushy if overcooked, unlike the white variety.

Do make sure to rinse your quinoa thoroughly before cooking it, as it is coated in a natural compound called saponins, which can impart a bitter flavor.

Quinoa Flour. Quinoa flour is made by grinding white quinoa, resulting in a versatile flour with a subtle nutty-earthy flavor. It works perfectly in the High-Protein Loaf Bread (page 48) and Quinoa Breakfast Bagels (page 72). Quinoa flour has a lower glycemic impact than wheat flour, so it won't cause the same blood sugar spikes. It's a good choice to increase your protein intake. You can buy it preground online or in health-food stores or grind your own.

Rolled Oats and Oat Flour. Oats and oat flour are naturally gluten-free options for baking and are staple ingredients in many of my recipes. However, it's crucial to be mindful of cross-contamination. Oats are often processed in facilities that also handle wheat, which may introduce traces of gluten. If you have celiac disease or are highly sensitive to gluten, always choose oat products labeled as certified gluten-free.

Another important consideration when purchasing oats or oat flour is the potential presence of glyphosate, the active ingredient in many herbicides, such as Roundup. Even organic products can sometimes be affected by glyphosate contamination through environmental drift. Since glyphosate has been linked to various health concerns, opting for oats that are certified glyphosate-free is a smart choice. Whether you buy conventional or organic oats, look for third-party certifications on the packaging to verify that the product meets these standards.

Salt. I am salt free because excess salt (sodium) intake is associated with various health issues. However, I include salt in my recipes in the amount that I think is reasonable to make them palatable for people who still use it. If, like me, you are salt free, you can simply omit it from the recipes. If you do consume salt, I suggest adding as little as necessary for your tastes, and to eventually titrate the amount down as low as possible. To reduce or eliminate salt from your diet, a healthier alternative is potassium chloride, which can be used as a salt substitute. I suggest using a brand that has the single ingredient, potassium chloride, to avoid unnecessary ingredients.

Sesame Seeds. I love using lightly toasted sesame seeds to add a subtle, sweet, and nutty flavor to dishes. You'll find them featured throughout this book, often as a garnish and occasionally as the star of the show, like in my

Sesame Date Cookies (page 236). While all varieties of sesame seeds are highly nutritious, black sesame seeds and unhulled white sesame seeds stand out as particularly rich sources of calcium.

Hulled white sesame seeds are widely available in most grocery stores. For unhulled black or white sesame seeds, try looking in health-food stores or online retailers. Black sesame seeds are also a staple in Japanese cuisine, so they can often be found in Japanese markets.

Spices. The secret to crafting delicious and flavorful dishes lies in the spices. The right combinations can transform any recipe, adding depth and character. However, recent studies have revealed that some spice brands may contain concerning levels of toxic heavy metals. To ensure both safety and quality, I recommend researching reputable brands. Additionally, selecting fresh spices is essential to unlocking their full flavor potential and enhancing your dishes.

KEY SPICES

- Black pepper (peppercorns and ground)
- Cinnamon (stick and ground)
- Cumin (ground)
- Curry powder
- Garlic granules
- Ginger (fresh and ground)
- Italian seasoning
- Onion granules
- Oregano (dried)
- Parsley (fresh and dried)
- Sweet paprika
- Smoked paprika
- Thyme (dried)
- Turmeric (fresh and ground)

SECONDARY SPICES

- Allspice (ground)
- Basil (dried)
- Cardamom (pods and ground)
- Cayenne pepper
- Chili flakes
- Cloves (whole and ground)
- Fennel (ground)
- Mustard (ground)

Sunflower Seeds (raw). Raw sunflower seeds are a great nut-free alternative to cashews. While their flavor is mild, they aren't quite as neutral as cashews. However, they still create a deliciously creamy base for recipes. One thing to keep in mind is that sunflower seeds tend to oxidize faster than cashews, which can slightly alter the color of sauces and dressings. On the plus side, sunflower seeds are more affordable and widely ava lable at most grocery stores, making them a convenient option.

Tahini. Tahini, essentially sesame seed butter, is a key ingredient in Middle Eastern cuisine and a staple in dishes like hummus (pages 67, 68). Beyond its traditional uses, I enjoy incorporating tahini into desserts and as a nut-free alternative to nut butters. I typically use raw tahini that is thicker in consistency, unless a recipe specifically calls for the runny variety.

Tiger Nut Flour. Tiger nut flour is a less common alternative to traditional flours. Despite its name, tiger nuts are not nuts; they're tubers grown in parts of Africa and Spain. When ground, tiger nuts produce a naturally sweet flour that works well as a substitute for almond flour, making it a great option for those with nut allergies. In recipes where tiger nut flour is a suitable replacement for almond flour, I've included specific notes for guidance. Additionally, because tiger nut flour is inherently sweet, you can reduce the amount of added sweetener in certain foods when using it. It's not easy to find in conventional grocery stores, but some health-food stores will carry it, and it is readily available online.

MAKE YOUR OWN PUMFU

- 1 pound pumpkin seeds, soaked for 8 or more hours
- 5 cups water

1. Drain the water from your soaked pumpkin seeds and give them a rinse. Combine the pumpkin seeds and fresh water in a blender (depending on the size of your blender, you may need to do this in two batches). Blend on high until the pumpkin seeds are completely smooth with no visible pieces remaining.

2. Pour the pumpkin seeds mixture into a nut milk bag and squeeze to drain your pumpkin seed milk into a bowl. This process can take some time but just keep squeezing. When you're done, you shouldn't be able to manually squeeze any more liquid from your pulp, and the pulp should resemble soft Play-Doh.

3. Allow the milk to rest for 20 to 30 minutes to let the starch settle. After 20 minutes, slowly pour the milk into a heavy-bottom pot, taking care not to disturb the settled starch. Heat the milk on high. Stir constantly with a flat-edged spatula to avoid sticking and scorching.

4. Once the pumpkin seed milk begins to get hot, it will start to curdle. Turn off the heat but keep your pot on the burner and continue to gently stir until all the curds have formed and the liquid is no longer cloudy. Remove from the burner.

5. Place a colander in a bowl and line the colander with cheesecloth. Using a slotted skimmer utensil, remove the curds from the pot and add them to the lined colander. Do this until you have removed all the curds.

6. Gather the sides of your cheesecloth and twist to gently squeeze out excess moisture from the curds. Empty the bowl if necessary.

7. Twist the top of the cheesecloth and place a heavy bowl of water or kitchen weight (about 5 pounds) on top of your curds. Allow the pumpkin seed tofu to press overnight in the fridge to get a firm tofu.

8. Use as you would regular tofu. Store in a sealed container in the fridge for up to 4 days.

Zero waste: Store the pulp in the freezer and add it to smoothies or salads. Use the liquid left over from straining the curds as a broth or to make muffins or pancakes.

Tofu and Soy-Free Alternatives. Tofu is a by-product of soy milk. It is made by heating soy milk and adding a coagulant. Traditionally, gypsum or nigari are the coagulants that are used, but lemon juice and vinegar work as well. The coagulant causes the milk to curdle, and those curds are strained and pressed into blocks. I try to avoid using commercially made tofu because of the defoaming agents used during the production process. When I do use tofu, I prefer to make my own or use other soy-free alternatives, like pumpkin seed tofu, sometimes called pumfu (page 23). Pumpkin seeds are high in protein, iron, and zinc, which make them a healthy addition to any diet.

JAVANT'S HOMEMADE VEGETABLE BROTH

- 4 garlic cloves
- 4 ounces button mushrooms
- 4 ounces shiitake mushrooms (dried or fresh)
- 2 carrots
- 2 sticks celery
- 1 onion
- 1 leek
- 8–10 cups water
- 1–2 tablespoons coconut aminos
- ¼ teaspoon ground black pepper
- 1-inch piece fresh ginger root (optional)
- ½-inch piece fresh turmeric root (optional)

1. Wash and roughly chop the vegetables. Feel free to throw in the peels and skins.
2. Combine all the ingredients in a large stockpot along with the water. The water level should be about 2 inches above the veggies.
3. Bring to a boil, then reduce the temperature to a simmer. Cover and cook on low for 3 to 6 hours.
4. Strain the broth and add to glass jars or freezer-safe containers. This will yield about 10 cups.
5. Store in the fridge for up to 4 days or in the freeze for up to 3 months.

Vanilla Extract. I always choose pure vanilla extract for cooking because artificial flavorings are made with chemicals and fall short in taste. While I prefer using pure vanilla bean powder for its rich flavor, it can be quite expensive and harder to find. For convenience, all the recipes in this book use pure vanilla extract, which is readily available in major grocery stores, health-food stores, and online.

Vegetable Broth. Vegetable broth is an excellent way to enhance the depth of flavor in soups, curries, and other dishes. It's also a versatile alternative for sautéing in oil-free cooking. When selecting vegetable broth, choose an option that is both oil-free and salt-free or that is low in sodium; there are a good number of quality packaged options available.

Walnuts (raw). Nuts in general have been shown in several studies to be health promoting, but walnuts may be the healthiest of them all. Compared to other popular nuts, walnuts are high in omega-3 and overall antioxidants. What I find particularly impressive is that eating walnuts has been shown to improve arterial function, which could potentially result in fewer heart attacks and strokes.

You will notice that I use walnuts as my nut of choice for many of the recipes in this book, not only because they are good for you, but also because they provide great flavor. If you have an allergy or sensitivity to walnuts, pecans are the next best option in dishes where the walnuts provide texture, like my HV Veggie Ground (page 30) and Veggie Sausage Ground (page 33) recipes.

Wheat-Free Pasta Alternatives. When it comes to pasta, my personal preference is one or two ingredient varieties made from beans and lentils. I steer clear of brands that include unnecessary additional ingredients. These simple, wholesome pastas are becoming increasingly accessible and can now be found in conventional grocery stores, health-food stores, and online.

Whole Psyllium Husks. Psyllium husks come from the outer layer of the *Plantago ovata* seed and are an excellent addition to gluten-free baking. I use them in my recipes as a binder. Beyond their functional role in cooking, they are rich in fiber and promote healthy gut bacteria. Please note that all the recipes in this book specifically call for whole psyllium husks, not psyllium husk powder, as the latter won't yield the desired results. You can find psyllium husks in health-food stores and online.

In addition to these ingredients, I recommend keeping your kitchen stocked with fresh vegetables and fruits and your favorite whole grains. Many of the fruits and vegetables featured in the Salads, Bowls, and Soups section (page 159) can be easily substituted with your preferred options. Similarly, you can swap your favorite whole grains into any recipe that calls for millet or quinoa, tailoring each dish to your taste.

KITCHEN TOOLS

If you want to save time and streamline your food prep, here are a couple of small appliances and kitchen tools worth investing in. If you're already well versed in plant-based cooking, chances are you already have many, or even all, of these tools!

Essentials

Food Processor. A high-quality food processor is an essential kitchen tool, second only to a blender in versatility. It makes creating many of the recipes in this book a breeze. In these recipes you will be using the S blade, but most food processors come with a selection of grating and slicing blades as well, which is a nice addition. If you plan on purchasing a food processor, I suggest getting one that holds at least 10 cups, so that you don't find yourself having to process in multiple batches.

High-Speed Blender. A good-quality, high-speed blender, such as a Vitamix, Ninja, or Nutribullet, is an essential tool for creating dressings, drinks, silky-smooth cheesecake, and puddings, making it an invaluable addition to the kitchen. The good news is that you no longer need to spend hundreds of dollars on top-of-the-line models like the Vitamix to achieve excellent results. Many reliable blenders are available for under $150, and if you wait for a sale, you may score an even better deal.

Worth Considering

Air Fryer. I don't use an air fryer often, but it can be a nice appliance to have when creating oil-free recipes. It enables you to create an even, crisp coating on foods with minimal time and effort.

Immersion Blender. A stainless-steel immersion blender is another handy addition to the kitchen. I love using it to blend hot dishes, like soups and sauces, directly in the pot for effortless preparation.

Nut Milk Bag. I consider a good-quality, cotton nut milk bag an important tool if you plan on making your own plant milks (page 20) or pumfu (page 23). I lean toward using an organic cotton nut milk bag, since nonorganic cotton is exposed to a lot of chemicals during growing and processing. You can find a good selection of both organic and nonorganic cotton nut milk bags online.

Cookware and Bakeware

Seasoned Cast-Iron Pan (12 inch). A quality well-seasoned cast-iron pan is my go-to for preparing many recipes, like crab cakes, burgers, and a variety of mushroom dishes. Having one will come in handy when making the recipes in this book.

Stainless-Steel Pots and Pans. I suggest having stainless-steel pots and pans in a few different sizes to prepare sauces, soups, and curries. Try to choose pots and pans with thick bottoms, as pots with thin bottoms are more likely to scorch.

Stainless-Steel Sauté Pan or Wok (3 quart). This is the type of pan I use to prepare my HV Veggie Ground (page 30), as its large, wide bottom is perfect for accommodating the generous quantity the recipe yields. I've also discovered that this pan works great for making curries and chili, offering plenty of space for ingredients to cook evenly.

OTHER COOKWARE USED IN THIS BOOK

Baking sheet, 18 x 13 inch
Cake pan, 9 inch
Cooling rack
Loaf pan, 9 x 5 inch
Muffin pan
Springform pan, 7 inch
Square pan, 8 inch

MYO STAPLES

Keeping some of these staples on hand makes creating healthy vegan meals a breeze. If you're looking for whole food alternatives to processed, store-bought veggie meats, cheeses, and breads, then this is the section for you. So turn the page and let me share with you the foundations to create your favorite traditional meals . . . healthy vegan style!

HV Veggie Ground

This universal replacement for ground beef is my most popular recipe, made of healthy, whole food ingredients and full of flavor. It's a base for my Teriyaki No-Meatballs (page 200) and Greek-Style Burger (page 157), but you can use it anytime you would typically use ground beef or a store-bought replacement. This recipe yields 10 cups, so I recommend freezing it in single-meal portions to have on hand for easy meal prep (see notes).

DIFFICULTY
Easy

MAKES
10 cups

Ingredients

- 1½ cups raw walnuts, soaked for 4–8 hours
- 1 medium head cauliflower, about 1 pound, chopped or processed to the size of cooked rice
- 2 medium carrots, peeled and grated or processed to resemble cauliflower rice
- 1 small red onion, peeled and chopped or processed finely
- 3 garlic cloves, minced
- 1 pound portobello mushrooms, chopped or processed coarsely (see notes)

Seasoning

- 2 tablespoons Italian seasoning
- 1 tablespoon sweet paprika
- 2 teaspoons rubbed sage
- 2 teaspoons garlic granules
- 2 teaspoons ground cumin
- 1 teaspoon dried thyme
- 1 teaspoon dried oregano
- 3 tablespoons tomato paste
- 3 teaspoons salt or to taste (optional)

Directions

1. Drain the walnuts, discard the soaking water, and set aside.
2. Heat a large, wide-bottom pan on high, one that yields at least 3 quarts. Put in the cauliflower, carrots, onion, garlic, and mushrooms and mix.
3. Cook for 5 to 10 minutes, or until all the water releases from the vegetables and mushrooms. Stir the vegetables occasionally as they cook and the water from the vegetables starts to evaporate.
4. Add all the spices and mix to combine. Continue to cook on high for another 10 minutes, or until all the water fully evaporates and no water remains at the bottom of the pan when mixed.
5. Add the drained walnuts to the food processor, and using an S blade, pulse into a coarse crumb.
6. Turn off the heat and add the chopped walnuts, tomato paste, and salt, if using. Mix thoroughly to combine.

Notes

MEAL PREP: Keep this HV Veggie Ground on hand for quick meal prep. Simply freeze it in 1- to 2-cup portions, thaw, and use as desired. Store in an airtight container in the fridge for up to 5 days or in the freezer for 2 months.

NUT REPLACEMENT: If you can't have walnuts, pecans are the next best option for this recipe.

NUT-FREE: Replace the walnuts with sunflower or pumpkin seeds.

MUSHROOM-FREE: Use an equal amount of canned or jarred young jackfruit to replace the mushrooms. Be sure to rinse and soak the jackfruit before using it to remove excess salt.

Use a knife and grater if you don't own a food processor.

Notes

MEAL PREP: Keep this Veggie Sausage Ground on hand for quick meal prep. Simply freeze it in 1- to 2-cup portions, thaw, and use as desired. Store in an airtight container in the fridge for up to 5 days or in the freezer for 2 months.

NUT REPLACEMENT: If you can't have walnuts, pecans are the next best option for this recipe.

NUT-FREE: Replace the walnuts with sunflower or pumpkin seeds.

MUSHROOM-FREE: Use an equal amount of canned or jarred young jackfruit to replace the mushrooms. Be sure to rinse and soak the jackfruit before using it to remove excess salt.

The chopping process can be done using a knife and grater if you don't own a food processor.

Veggie Sausage Ground

Healthier, plant-based eating doesn't mean leaving sausage behind. This Veggie Sausage Ground has a base similar to my HV Veggie Ground, but the prominent flavors of sage, fennel, and red chili flakes, offset with a hint of sweetness from the coconut aminos, really make it stand out. You can use this to create other delicious meals like my Breakfast Sausage Patties (page 86) or add it to any dishes that would typically call for ground sausage.

DIFFICULTY
Easy

MAKES
7 cups

Ingredients

- 1½ cups raw walnuts, soaked for 4–8 hours
- 1 medium head cauliflower, about 1 pound, chopped or processed to the size of cooked rice
- 1 pound white mushrooms, chopped or processed coarsely (see notes)
- 1 small yellow onion, chopped or processed finely
- 2 garlic cloves

Seasoning

- 1¼ teaspoons garlic granules
- 3 tablespoons dried sage
- 1½ teaspoons dried thyme
- ¼ teaspoon ground nutmeg
- 2 tablespoons ground fennel
- ½–¾ teaspoon chili flakes
- ½ teaspoon ground black pepper
- 3 tablespoons coconut aminos
- 3 tablespoons tomato paste
- 1½ teaspoons salt or to taste (optional)

Directions

1. Drain the walnuts and discard the soaking water. Coarsely chop the walnuts and set aside.
2. Heat a large, wide-bottom pan on high.
3. Put in the cauliflower, mushrooms, onion, and garlic and mix. Cook for 5 to 10 minutes, or until all the water releases from the vegetables and mushrooms. Stir the vegetables occasionally as they cook and the water from the vegetables starts to evaporate.
4. Add all the spices and mix to combine. Continue to cook on high for another 10 minutes, or until all the water fully evaporates and no water remains at the bottom of the pan when mixed.
5. Add the coconut aminos and cook for another 3 to 5 minutes, or until the liquid has evaporated. The mixture is done cooking when there is no longer any moisture at the bottom of the pan; you will hear the vegetables sizzling when you stir them.
6. Add the drained walnuts to the food processor, and using an S blade, pulse into a coarse crumb.
7. Turn off the heat and add the chopped walnuts, tomato paste, and salt, if using. Mix thoroughly to combine.

Chick'n-Style Mushrooms

DIFFICULTY
Easy

MAKES
2 cups

Once I learned about the amazing health benefits of mushrooms, I made a conscious decision to include them in my diet daily. While all mushrooms are healthy, lion's mane and oyster mushrooms have some unique benefits. Oyster mushrooms are known for their ability to support cardiovascular and metabolic health, and lion's mane mushrooms are known for their cognitive and nerve regeneration benefits, and they can both be used interchangeably in this recipe.

When I first cooked with oyster and lion's mane mushrooms, I was blown away by their meaty texture. After experimenting with different flavor profiles, it became clear that, with the right seasoning and technique, these mushrooms could easily win over even the most devoted chicken lover. Try either of the spice blends below to prepare them, then toss into your favorite casseroles (like my No-Chick'n Enchilada Casserole on page 211), tacos, pizzas, or wraps (especially my No-Chick'n Caesar Wrap on page 138).

Ingredients

1½ pounds fresh lion's mane or oyster mushrooms

2 tablespoons coconut aminos

BASIC SEASONING

1 teaspoon dried parsley

¼ teaspoon dried thyme

¼ teaspoon dried oregano

½ teaspoon smoked paprika

½ teaspoon garlic granules

¼ teaspoon onion granules

¼ teaspoon ground mustard

Salt to taste

MEXICAN-STYLE SEASONING

1 teaspoon garlic granules

1 teaspoon sweet paprika

1 teaspoon ground cumin

½ teaspoon onion granules

½ teaspoon smoked paprika

½ teaspoon dried oregano

Salt to taste

¼ teaspoon chipotle seasoning (optional)

Directions

① Cut any hard stem from the base of the mushrooms. Using your hands, pull the mushrooms into larger pieces (about 1½ inches).

② Put the mushrooms in a 12-inch pan on medium-high heat. Cook the mushrooms for 1 to 3 minutes, or until their water begins to release.

③ Increase the heat to high. Place a heavy-bottom cast-iron pan or burger press on top of the mushrooms. Press down to

(recipe continues)

Chick'n-Style Mushrooms (continued)

encourage the water in the mushrooms to release and cook off, creating a denser texture. Mix the mushrooms every 2 to 3 minutes. Continue to press in between mixing until almost all the water has evaporated. This process can take 5 to 10 minutes, until the mushrooms start to brown.

(4) Add the coconut aminos and seasonings (either basic or Mexican-style), and continue to cook for an additional 5 to 10 minutes, or until the water has cooked off.

Notes

Store in the fridge for up to 3 days.

MUSHROOM-FREE: Use an equal amount of canned or jarred young jackfruit. Be sure to rinse and soak the jackfruit before using it to remove excess salt.

Easy Cheese Sauce

For many people, giving up cheese is not something they want to consider. The good news is that you can give up dairy and still have a rich, creamy sauce. The secret to the creaminess here is cashews, but I have included a nut-free option if you would like an alternative. Either way you make it, you will love the silky, smooth cheesiness that it brings to any dish. Use this cheese sauce in dishes like my Veggie Sausage Lasagna (page 198), No-Chick'n Enchilada Casserole (page 211), or my Sweet Potato Chili Cheese Fries (page 187).

DIFFICULTY
Easy

MAKES
1½ cups

Ingredients

1 cup raw cashews, soaked for 4–8 hours

2 teaspoons lemon juice

½ cup water

2 tablespoons nutritional yeast

¼ teaspoon salt or to taste

¼ teaspoon ground black pepper (optional)

¼ teaspoon garlic granules (optional)

Directions

1. Drain the cashews and discard the soaking water.
2. Combine all the ingredients in a high-speed blender and blend until smooth.

Notes

Store your cheese sauce in an airtight container in the fridge for up to 5 days.

Use 1 tablespoon of miso paste to replace nutritional yeast.

NUT-FREE: Replace the cashews with ½ cup of cannellini beans and ½ cup of raw sunflower seeds.

Easy Cheese Sauce
(page 37)

Classic Sour Cream
(page 40)

Simple Tomato Sauce
(page 41)

MaYO
(page 40)

MaYO: Make Your Own Mayo

This oil-free, vegan mayo was one of the first recipes I came up with. This is my original recipe made with cashews, but my nut-free version is just as good. Try this on sandwiches, as a base for dips, or use it to make my No-Crab Cakes (page 190).

DIFFICULTY
Easy

MAKES
1½ cups

Ingredients

- 1 cup raw cashews, soaked for 4–8 hours
- ¼–½ cup water
- 1 tablespoon lemon juice
- 1 tablespoon apple cider vinegar
- 1 teaspoon Dijon mustard
- 1 teaspoon garlic granules
- ½ teaspoon onion granules
- ½ teaspoon salt or to taste

Directions

1. Drain the cashews and discard the soaking water.
2. Combine all the ingredients except the water in a high-speed blender and blend. Add the water gradually. Continue to blend until a smooth mayo-like consistency is reached.

Notes

Store your mayo in an airtight container in the fridge for up to 5 days.

NUT-FREE: Replace the cashews with ½ cup of canned cannellini beans (drained and rinsed) and ½ cup of raw sunflower seeds. Start by adding 3 tablespoons of water and adjust as needed.

Classic Sour Cream

You can make your own sour cream with ingredients you probably already have on hand. Not only is this super easy, but this vegan sour cream also has the same thick and creamy consistency you'd typically expect from dairy-based sour cream, as well as the same tang. You can use it in any dish you'd like to add a rich, tangy flavor; it's also a great complement to dishes like my Three-Bean Chili (page 189), Chickpea Tacos (page 153), and Nacho Salad Bowl (page 164).

DIFFICULTY
Easy

MAKES
2 cups

Ingredients

- 1½ cups raw cashews, soaked for 4–8 hours
- ¾ cup water
- 2 tablespoons lemon juice
- 2 teaspoons apple cider vinegar
- ½ teaspoon salt

Directions

1. Drain the cashews and discard the soaking water.
2. Combine all the ingredients in a high-speed blender and blend until smooth. Chill in the refrigerator for 2 or more hours.

Note

Store in an airtight container in the fridge for up to 5 days or in the freezer for up to 1 month.

Sub up to half a cup of cashews with hemp hearts to improve the omega profile.

Simple Tomato Sauce

Guess what? It turns out you don't have to let your pasta sauce simmer for five hours to get great results. You can make this simple and flavorful tomato sauce in less than thirty minutes. You can double the batch to freeze (see notes); this is a great one to have on hand—you can use this sauce to create everything from Veggie Sausage Lasagna (page 198) to stuffed peppers, so there's no reason not to make your own!

DIFFICULTY
Easy

MAKES
4 cups

Ingredients

¼ cup vegetable broth or water

3 garlic cloves, crushed

30 ounces canned or jarred tomato purée (see notes)

3 teaspoons dried basil

¾ teaspoon dried oregano

¾ teaspoon salt or to taste

Ground black pepper to taste

1. Pour the vegetable broth in a saucepan and heat on medium until the liquid is lightly simmering.
2. Add the garlic and let simmer for 2 minutes.
3. Add the tomato purée and spices.
4. Cover and simmer on low for 20 minutes until the sauce thickens slightly.

Notes

Store single-meal portions in the freezer for quick meal prep.

You may also blend canned or jarred whole tomatoes to make this sauce. Since tomatoes are acidic and can have a reaction with the metal in cans, I prefer to purchase tomatoes in a glass jar.

Date Paste

I stopped eating refined sugar in 2011. Now I sweeten everything from sauces to desserts with dates: whole dates, date paste, date sugar, and occasionally date syrup. Dates are a much healthier sweetener than refined sugars because they contain fiber, vitamins, minerals, antioxidants, and phytochemicals. Also, because dates contain fiber, the sugar from dates is absorbed much slower than refined sugar, resulting in lower blood sugar spikes. I keep this basic paste on hand and use it in everything from my breakfast cookies (pages 103–106) to my Apple Crumb Pie (page 261) and Teriyaki Sauce (page 60). You can use it as a swap for sugar in many recipes or anytime you want to add a little sweetness. On its own it tastes like caramel . . . you've been warned!

DIFFICULTY
Easy

MAKES
1 cup

Ingredients

12 Medjool dates, pitted

2/3 cup water

Directions

Combine the dates and water in a high-speed blender and blend until smooth.

Notes

Store your date paste in an airtight container for up to 7 days in the refrigerator.

If your dates are somewhat dry, you can let them soak in hot water for an hour before blending.

Extra Crunchy Wheat-Free Breadcrumbs (page 47)

Wheat-Free Breadcrumbs
(page 46)

Wheat-Free Breadcrumbs

Breadcrumbs are a basic ingredient in so many recipes, but when following a diet free of wheat and rice, they can be difficult to substitute. These almond flour breadcrumbs are a delicious swap—they work perfectly for both breading and binding. I use them in my No-Crab Cakes (page 190), Sticky Teriyaki Cauliflower Wings (page 180), and Mango Buffalo Mushroom Wings (page 183). You can use them as a one-to-one replacement anytime you need breadcrumbs.

DIFFICULTY
Easy

MAKES
1 cup

Ingredients

1 cup almond flour

2 teaspoons ground flaxseed

½ teaspoon ground black pepper

½ teaspoon garlic granules

½ ground sweet or smoked paprika

1 teaspoon salt or to taste

2 tablespoons water

Notes

Store completely dry crumbs in an airtight container for up to a week.

For recipes like my Sticky Teriyaki Cauliflower Wings (page 180) and Mango Buffalo Mushroom Wings (page 183), I grind my crumbs even finer, as I find the finer crumbs coat and stick better.

NUT-FREE: Use tiger nut flour. Be careful to watch it closely while heating as I find the tiger nut crumbs can burn if you're not careful.

Directions

1. Whisk together the dry ingredients in a bowl. Add the water slowly and mix to create a crumbly texture.

2. Transfer the mixture to a skillet on medium-low heat. Using a spatula, mix and break down the crumbs as they dry. The crumbs will begin to dry out and won't stick due to the natural oils releasing.

3. Reduce the temperature to just above low and continue to dry out the mixture, using the spatula to stir the crumbs and taking care not to burn them. This drying-out process can take up to 30 minutes to complete.

4. Once your crumbs are completely dry, remove the pan from the heat and allow them to cool completely. Pulse in a processor to achieve the desired crumb.

Extra Crunchy Wheat-Free Breadcrumbs

Packed with protein and fiber, chickpeas are a versatile and hearty legume. But did you know they can also make a perfect wheat- and nut-free breadcrumb alternative? So easy to make, they add that extra layer of crunchy exterior to my No-Crab Cakes (page 190), Sticky Teriyaki Cauliflower Wings (page 180), and Mango Buffalo Mushroom Wings (page 183). Note that due to their water content, these do take longer to dry than nut-flour-based breadcrumbs, but it's worth the extra time.

DIFFICULTY
Easy

MAKES
1 cup

Ingredients

2⅔ cups cooked chickpeas, or 2 (15-ounce) cans chickpeas, drained and rinsed

½ teaspoon garlic granules

½ teaspoon onion granules

1 teaspoon dried parsley

½ teaspoon sweet paprika

1 teaspoon salt or to taste

Note

These crumbs store well in an airtight container for up to 1 week.

Directions

1. Preheat the oven to 350°F.
2. Pulse the chickpeas in a food processor to create a crumbly texture; do not overprocess.
3. Spread on a baking sheet. Sprinkle with the spices and mix.
4. Bake for 30 to 45 minutes, or until completely dry. Mix periodically. The crumbs are ready when they are dry and crunchy to the touch.
5. Allow the crumbs to cool before using or storing.

High-Protein Loaf Bread

Making your own bread may sound like a time-consuming challenge, but this loaf is much faster and easier than making a traditional loaf of bread. Quinoa flour adds a boost of plant protein, and psyllium husks help to bind the dough while promoting gut health. This bread is moist and hearty with a springy texture, which I really enjoy. This bread is a great choice for breakfast toast or used to make my No-Tuna Salad Sandwich (page 146) or an HV BLT (page 145).

DIFFICULTY
Medium

MAKES
1 loaf

Ingredients

DRY

- 3 cups quinoa flour (400 grams)
- 2½ teaspoons baking powder (8 grams)
- ½ teaspoon baking soda (4 grams)
- 1 tablespoon ground flaxseed or ground chia seeds (7 grams)
- ¾ teaspoon salt or to taste (5 grams)

WET

- 2½ cups water (600 milliliters)
- 1 tablespoon apple cider vinegar (16 milliliters)
- 1–2 tablespoons date syrup or date paste (page 43)
- ⅓ scant cup whole psyllium husks (25 grams) (see notes)

OPTIONAL TOPPING

- Hemp hearts

Directions

1. Preheat the oven to 350°F. Prepare a 9 x 5-inch loaf pan by dusting the bottom with quinoa flour or lining it with parchment paper.
2. In a bowl, whisk together the dry ingredients.
3. In a separate bowl, whisk together the wet ingredients, including the psyllium husks. Let rest for 5 to 10 minutes until the wet mixture has thickened into a gel consistency; it will still be pourable.
4. Combine the wet and dry ingredients. I prefer using a silicone spatula to mix this dough until it has almost come together. The dough will be soft, moist, and slightly sticky.
5. Once the dough has come together, wet your hands to keep the dough from sticking. Add the dough to your loaf pan. Smooth the top and any cracks by rubbing them with your wet hands. Do not compact or press down on the dough or it will produce a denser loaf. Top with a generous layer of hemp hearts, if using.
6. Bake for 100 minutes, or until golden.
7. Immediately lift the loaf out of the pan by the edges of the parchment paper and discard the paper. Cool the loaf on a rack completely before cutting.

Notes

Store the loaf in an airtight container on the counter for up to 2 days or slice and freeze for up to 1 month.

Make sure to use whole psyllium husks for this recipe; using psyllium husk powder will result in a gummy texture.

Soft Almond Flatbread

I have made—and eaten—so many wheat-free flatbreads, but this one is still my favorite. It's soft in texture, yet holds up well to being rolled and wrapped. Once you get the hang of making these, you can roll them thicker (for heartier fillings) or thinner (for a tortilla-like dish), depending on what you're using them for. I roll them thicker when making my No-Meatball Gyro (page 149) and smaller and thinner for my Chickpea Tacos (page 153). Take a simple vegetable wrap up a notch by adding one or more of the optional seasonings to your flatbread.

DIFFICULTY
Easy

MAKES
4 flatbreads

Ingredients

1 cup almond flour

3 tablespoons whole psyllium husks (see notes)

¼ teaspoon salt or to taste

¼ teaspoon garlic granules, Italian seasoning, dried oregano, or another seasoning of choice (optional)

½ cup water

Notes

Store between parchment paper in an airtight container for up to 3 days.

Make sure to use whole psyllium husks for this recipe. Using psyllium husk powder will result in a gummy texture.

NUT-FREE: Substitute tiger nut flour for the almond flour and use ½ tablespoon more of psyllium husks.

Directions

1. Preheat the oven to 425°F. Once the oven is heated, put a baking sheet in the oven to heat up.
2. In a bowl, combine the almond flour, psyllium husks, salt, and seasoning. Add the water and mix until combined. Let sit for 5 minutes.
3. When the dough mixture has absorbed the water, divide into 4 equal portions and roll into balls.
4. Place a 10-inch piece of parchment paper on the counter and drop one of the balls on top; top with a second piece of parchment paper and roll into a circle between 1⁄16 and ⅛ inch thick and 7 to 8 inches round. Remove the top layer of parchment paper but keep the rolled dough on the bottom piece.
5. Place the parchment paper with the rolled dough onto the heated baking sheet in the oven. Bake for 3 to 4 minutes, or a minute longer for a thicker flatbread. Carefully remove the parchment paper with the cooked flatbread. Transfer to a plate. Continue this process for the remaining dough.

Gluten-Free Millet Burger Buns

Most gluten-free burger buns are full of oil and additives. This bun recipe uses nutrient-dense millet flour for a flavor that is mild and neutral with a soft, classic bun texture—the perfect resting place for a delicious Greek-Style Burger (page 157), a Better Bacon Cheeseburger (page 154), or anytime you need a bun. Bonus: This recipe can also be used to make a delicious soft sandwich loaf (see notes).

DIFFICULTY
Easy

MAKES
6 buns

Ingredients

DRY

2½ cups millet flour (400 grams) (see notes)

2½ teaspoons baking powder (8 grams)

½ teaspoon baking soda (4 grams)

¾ teaspoon salt or to taste (5 grams)

2 tablespoons ground flaxseed or ground chia seeds (14 grams)

WET

2½ cups water (600 milliliters)

1 tablespoon apple cider vinegar (16 milliliters)

2 tablespoons date syrup or date paste (page 43)

⅓ cup whole psyllium husks (30 grams) (see notes)

OPTIONAL TOPPING

Sesame seeds

Directions

1. Preheat the oven to 350°F. If you don't have a bun pan, line a baking sheet with parchment paper and set aside.
2. In a bowl, whisk together the dry ingredients.
3. In a separate bowl, whisk together the wet ingredients and the psyllium husks. Let rest for 5 minutes until it has a gel-like consistency.
4. Using a spatula, combine the wet and dry ingredients.
5. Wet your hands and add one-sixth of the dough to each section of the bun pan, or form into buns on the parchment-lined baking sheet. Top with sesame seeds, if using. Bake for 50 to 60 minutes, or until slightly golden brown.
6. Remove from the oven and allow to cool completely before cutting.

Notes

These buns can be stored in an airtight container for up to 3 days on the counter or up to 1 month in the freezer.

This recipe makes a delicious, soft, millet loaf bread. Just add the dough to a 9 x 5-inch loaf pan and bake for 80 minutes.

Make your own millet flour by grinding the whole millet in a high-speed blender.

Make sure to use whole psyllium husks for this recipe. Using psyllium husk powder will result in a gummy texture.

Top these buns with your choice of seeds, like sesame seeds or even Everything Seasoning to take them to the next level.

SAUCES, DRESSINGS, AND DIPS

Healthy sauces are an important part of the Make Your Own cooking approach. Good sauces are an excellent way to add five-star flavors to any ordinary dish. My sauces are amazingly delicious and super healthy because I use a variety of nutritious whole foods, like beans, nuts, and seeds, to replace oil, and dates to replace refined sugar. They are great as a salad dressing or dip, or to put on a sandwich or over pasta. Most of us have a favorite sauce that we purchase, and there's a good chance that I offer a healthier version that you can make yourself. The best part of all is that most of my sauces can be made in five minutes or less!

Sweet Cherry BBQ Sauce

Finding an oil-free, refined-sugar-free BBQ sauce is not an easy feat. Trust me, I've tried—so I made my own. This BBQ sauce has the perfect balance of tang and sweetness. It's my go-to sauce, especially on my Pulled BBQ Jackfruit Sandwich (page 142). Use it anytime you want to level up a sandwich or dish to BBQ status.

DIFFICULTY
Easy

MAKES
3 cups

Ingredients

¼ cup vegetable broth or water

1 medium onion, chopped

2 garlic cloves, minced

2 cups frozen dark sweet cherries, pitted

1 cup tomato paste

⅓ cup plus 1 tablespoon date syrup

¼ cup plus 1 tablespoon apple cider vinegar

¼ teaspoon onion granules

½ teaspoon garlic granules

2 tablespoons coconut aminos

2 tablespoons Dijon mustard

½ teaspoon smoked paprika

½ teaspoon ground black pepper

Directions

(1) Heat the vegetable broth in a saucepan on medium-high for 1 to 2 minutes, or until lightly simmering.

(2) Add the onion and garlic and cook until soft, for about 5 minutes.

(3) Add the remaining ingredients and gently simmer for 15 to 20 minutes, or until the cherries have mostly broken down.

(4) Allow to cool completely and blend in a high-speed blender until smooth.

Note

Store this BBQ sauce in an airtight container in the fridge for up to 1 week or in the freezer for up to 3 months.

Spicy Mango Buffalo Sauce

You can't go wrong with keeping buffalo sauce on hand. I wanted to create an easy spin on a traditional buffalo sauce, but one with some more substance and sweetness. I love mangoes, so it was a no-brainer for me to try them first; I was not disappointed, and I don't think you will be either. This buffalo sauce is perfectly sweet and spicy, so go ahead and try it in my Mango Buffalo Mushroom Wings (page 183) or smother it on some roasted veggies (I like cauliflower) or any sandwich that needs a buffalo kick.

DIFFICULTY
Easy

MAKES
2 cups

Ingredients

¼ cup raw cashews, soaked for 4–8 hours

¼ cup hot sauce, adjust to taste

½ cup water

2 mangoes, pitted, peeled, and diced

½ cup water

2 tablespoons date syrup (see notes)

2 teaspoons apple cider vinegar

1 tablespoon coconut aminos

1 teaspoon garlic granules

Directions

1. Drain the cashews, discard the soaking water, and set aside.
2. Combine all the ingredients except for the cashews in a saucepan and simmer for 10 minutes, or until the mango pieces are soft and slightly broken down.
3. Add the cashews. Let cool completely and then add to a high-speed blender and blend until smooth.

Notes

Store in an airtight container in the fridge for up to 1 week or in the freezer for up to 3 months.

You may substitute the date syrup with 3 tablespoons of date paste (page 43).

Jerk Sauce
(page 61)
Spicy Mango Buffalo Sauce
(page 57)
Teriyaki Sauce
(page 60)

Sweet Cherry BBQ Sauce
(page 56)

Jalapeño Lime Sauce
(page 60)

Teriyaki Sauce

DIFFICULTY
Easy

MAKES
2 cups

Most commercial teriyaki sauces are full of oil and refined sugar. This version uses pineapple juice and date paste for natural sweetness, balanced out with ginger and vinegar—it packs all the delicious flavor, with the healthy additions of fresh garlic and ginger. You'll want to cover vegetables, grains, and noodles with it. Not sure where to start? Check out my Teriyaki No-Meatballs (page 200) for dinner inspiration!

Ingredients

- ¾ cup unsweetened pineapple juice (see notes)
- ¼ cup coconut aminos
- ⅓ cup unsweetened ketchup, or tomato paste
- ½ cup date paste (page 43)
- 2 tablespoons apple cider vinegar
- 1½ tablespoons grated fresh ginger
- 3 garlic cloves, minced
- Chili flakes to taste

Directions

Combine the ingredients in a saucepan and simmer on low for 5 to 10 minutes, or until slightly thickened.

Notes

Store in an airtight container in the fridge for up to 5 days or in the freezer for up to 3 months.

Use an equal amount of whole blended pineapple instead of juice to retain the fiber and reduce blood sugar spikes.

Jalapeño Lime Sauce

DIFFICULTY
Easy

MAKES
1½ cups

You really can't go wrong with a combination of jalapeño and lime. This sauce is creamy and tangy, with a mild kick, and of course I added a date for a subtle sweetness. This sauce is delicious on a variety of wraps, salads, or even as a dip for your favorite veggies. You'll see it used on my Chickpea Tacos (page 153) and my Island-Style Jerk Pulled Mushroom Wrap (page 141).

Ingredients

- ½ cup raw cashews, soaked for 4–8 hours
- ½ cup hemp hearts
- ½ cup water
- 2 teaspoons apple cider vinegar
- 1 lime, juiced
- 2 garlic cloves
- 1 jalapeño, stem and seeds removed
- 1 Medjool date, pitted
- 1 teaspoon salt or to taste
- ⅓ cup cilantro, packed

Directions

① Drain the cashews and discard the soaking water.

② Combine all the ingredients in a high-speed blender and blend until smooth.

Note

Store in an airtight container in the fridge for up to 3 days or in the freezer for up to 1 month.

NUT-FREE: Use raw sunflower seeds to replace the cashews.

Jerk Sauce

This jerk sauce is both sweet and spicy, with the traditional Jamaican flavors of allspice and thyme. The sweetness comes from the dates and pineapple juice. If you want to tone down the heat level, you can use jalapeño instead of the traditional Scotch bonnet peppers. This sauce is a great complement to dishes including jackfruit, mushrooms, eggplant, and cauliflower. Not sure where to start? Check out my Island-Style Jerk Pulled Mushroom Wrap (page 141).

DIFFICULTY
Easy

MAKES
1½ cups

Ingredients

5 green onions

3 garlic cloves

1-inch piece fresh ginger root

1½ teaspoons ground allspice

1½ teaspoons dried thyme

½ teaspoon ground cinnamon

¼ teaspoon nutmeg

¼ cup coconut aminos

½ cup unsweetened pineapple juice (see notes)

6–8 Medjool dates, pitted

¼ cup water

1 Scotch bonnet or habañero pepper, seeded (see notes)

1 lime, juiced

Salt as needed

Directions

Combine all the ingredients in a high-speed blender and blend until smooth.

Notes

Store in an airtight container in the fridge for up to 1 week or in the freezer for up to 3 months.

Replace the pineapple juice with whole blended pineapple to retain the fiber and reduce blood sugar spikes.

If you are sensitive to spicy heat, I recommend reducing or omitting the Scotch bonnet from the recipe. You can also use the milder jalapeño pepper to replace the Scotch bonnet.

Creamy Caesar Dressing

I may be biased but hear me out: This is the best Caesar dressing. Whether you're using cashews or my nut-free option to make this dressing, the result is a decadent creamy base. Dulse flakes stand in for anchovies to give that subtle sea taste of traditional Caesar dressings. I use this on salads, burgers, and wraps like my No-Chick'n Caesar Wrap (page 138). Just want a simple Caesar salad? Go ahead and drench your favorite greens with this one!

DIFFICULTY
Easy

MAKES
1 cup

Ingredients

½ cup raw cashews, soaked for 4–8 hours

¼ cup plus 3 tablespoons water

2 tablespoons lemon juice

2 tablespoons nutritional yeast

¼ teaspoon dulse flakes

½ teaspoon dried parsley

2 garlic cloves

1 Medjool date, pitted

¼ teaspoon ground black pepper

1 teaspoon salt or to taste

Directions

① Drain the cashews and discard the soaking water.

② Combine all the ingredients in a high-speed blender and blend until smooth.

Notes

Store in an airtight container in the fridge for 3 to 5 days or in the freezer for up to 1 month.

NUT-FREE: Replace the cashews with ½ cup of canned cannellini beans and ½ cup of raw sunflower seeds. Since cannellini beans contain water, you can reduce the water as needed.

Tzatziki Sauce

This garlicky cucumber sauce traditionally is made using yogurt, but here I'm using cashews to create the thick creaminess. With the addition of fresh cucumber and dill, you really can't go wrong. I love this stuff on everything, particularly my Greek-Style Burger (page 157) and my No-Meatball Gyro (page 149). I also recommend trying this as a dip for your favorite veggies and snacks. Truthfully, I could eat a whole bowl of this stuff by the spoonful!

DIFFICULTY
Easy

MAKES
2½ cups

Ingredients

1 cup raw cashews, soaked for 4–8 hours

½ large English cucumber, peeled and grated

2 tablespoons chopped fresh dill

½–¾ cup water (see notes)

1½ tablespoons lemon juice

½ tablespoon apple cider vinegar

2 garlic cloves, minced

½ teaspoon salt

Ground black pepper to taste

Notes

Store in an airtight container in the fridge for up to 5 days.

Don't waste the water from the squeezed cucumber. Use it to replace all or some of the water in this recipe.

NUT-FREE: Replace the cashews with raw sunflower seeds.

Directions

1. Drain the cashews, discard the soaking water, and set aside.
2. With your hands, gently squeeze the grated cucumber over a small bowl to remove excess liquid. I like to do this with a stainless-steel mesh strainer. Reserve the cucumber water and set aside the grated cucumber.
3. Set aside the dill.
4. In a high-speed blender, combine all the other ingredients and blend until smooth.
5. Transfer to a bowl and add the grated cucumber and fresh dill. Mix to combine.

Sweet Dijon Dressing
(page 66)
Mango Vinaigrette
(page 66)
Creamy Dill Ranch
Dressing (page 65)
Tzatziki Sauce
(page 63)
Creamy Caesar Dressing
(page 62)

Creamy Dill Ranch Dressing

In my unofficial survey, it seems that ranch is hands-down America's favorite dressing. My slightly sweet and tangy version turns the most basic bowl of vegetables into a delicious and satisfying dish. Choose it as the perfect complement to a platter of vegetables or, even better, a platter of my Mango Buffalo Mushroom Wings (page 183).

DIFFICULTY
Easy

MAKES
1½ cups

Ingredients

- 1 cup raw cashews, soaked for 4–8 hours
- ½ cup hemp hearts
- ¾ cup water
- 2 tablespoons apple cider vinegar
- 1 teaspoon garlic granules
- 1 teaspoon onion granules
- ¼ cup fresh dill (see notes)
- 1 Medjool date, pitted
- 1 teaspoon salt or to taste

Directions

(1) Drain the cashews and discard the soaking water.

(2) Combine all the ingredients in a high-speed blender and blend until smooth.

Notes

Store in an airtight container in the fridge for up to 5 days or in the freezer for up to 1 month.

Switch the flavor up by using fresh chives to replace the dill.

NUT-FREE: Replace the cashews with ½ cup of cannellini beans, drained and rinsed, and ½ cup of raw sunflower seeds. Since cannellini beans contain water, start with 3 tablespoons of water and adjust as needed.

Mango Vinaigrette

DIFFICULTY
Easy

MAKES
1 cup

Mango is one of my favorite flavors—it pairs well with both sweet and savory dishes. This refreshing dressing is reminiscent of classic American-style French dressing. Drizzle it over your favorite greens for a burst of tanginess and surprising tropical sweetness.

Ingredients

- 1 mango, peeled and pitted
- 1 tablespoon apple cider vinegar
- 1 tablespoon coconut aminos
- ½ teaspoon smoked paprika
- ½ cup water

Directions

Combine all the ingredients in a high-speed blender and blend until smooth.

Note

Store in an airtight container in the fridge for up to 3 days or in the freezer for up to 1 month.

Sweet Dijon Dressing

DIFFICULTY
Easy

MAKES
1½ cups

Do you love a good honey-mustard dressing but had to give it up? This Dijon dressing is here to come to the rescue. Instead of oil, I use walnuts, which are rich in omega-3 fatty acids and antioxidants, to create the creamy base, and I replace high-glycemic honey with my favorite whole food sweetener, dates. This dressing takes five minutes to throw together and never disappoints!

Ingredients

- 2 tablespoons apple cider vinegar
- 2 tablespoons Dijon mustard
- ¾ cup water
- ½ cup walnuts
- 5 Medjool dates, pitted

Directions

Combine all the ingredients in a high-speed blender and blend until smooth.

Note

Store in an airtight container in the fridge for up to 1 week or in the freezer for up to 1 month.

Cilantro Pea Pesto

Most pesto recipes call for oil and dairy; this pesto is full of healthy plant proteins. The secret ingredients? Peas and pumpkin seeds combined with fresh cilantro result in this delicious pesto sauce with a twist! It works perfectly over pasta and pizza and in sandwiches.

DIFFICULTY
Easy

MAKES
2 cups

Ingredients

- 1½ cups green peas
- 1 packed cup cilantro
- 2 garlic cloves
- 4 tablespoons nutritional yeast
- ½ lemon, juiced
- ¾ cup pumpkin seeds
- 1 teaspoon salt or to taste
- ½ cup water

Directions

Combine all the ingredients in a food processor and blend. Add small amounts of water to adjust the consistency as needed.

Note

This pesto can be stored in the fridge for up to 3 days but is best when eaten fresh.

Pesto Hummus

I'm always looking for ways to combine different varieties of healthy foods into my recipes to make it easier for others to eat well. One easy way to do that is to play with flavor combinations. Who doesn't love a good fresh basil pesto? I know I do, so marrying hummus and pesto for this recipe is a match made in heaven!

DIFFICULTY
Easy

MAKES
2 cups

Ingredients

- 1⅓ cups cooked chickpeas, or 1 (15-ounce) can chickpeas, drained and rinsed
- 1 cup packed fresh basil
- 2 garlic cloves
- 3 tablespoons tahini
- 2 tablespoons nutritional yeast
- ½ lemon, juiced
- ½ teaspoon salt or to taste
- ⅓ cup water or more as needed

Directions

Combine all the ingredients in a food processor. Process for at least 60 seconds for a nice smooth consistency. For a thicker hummus, start with a ¼ cup of water and add small amounts to adjust the consistency.

Note

Store in an airtight container in the fridge for up to 3 days.

Sweet Potato Hummus

Beans are super healthy; not only are they full of fiber and protein, but they are also great for helping regulate blood sugar and supporting heart and gut health among other things. Hummus is a great way to eat beans daily. This take on hummus includes a few surprise ingredients: sweet potatoes, cinnamon, and miso. Growing up in the South, I've had a lifelong love for sweet potatoes. Their sweet creaminess and nutrient density complement the classic chickpeas while cinnamon and miso up the flavor with a hint of sweet umami.

DIFFICULTY
Easy

MAKES
3 cups

Ingredients

1 medium sweet potato

1⅓ cups cooked chickpeas, or 1 (15-ounce) can chickpeas, drained and rinsed

1 garlic clove

½ lemon, juiced

3 tablespoons tahini

¼ teaspoon ground cinnamon

1 tablespoon miso paste

Salt to taste

¼–½ cup water

Directions

1. Bake the sweet potato at 400°F for 40 minutes, or until a fork inserts with ease.
2. Cool the sweet potato, then peel it.
3. Combine all the ingredients in a food processor. Process for at least 60 seconds for a nice smooth consistency.

Note

Store in an airtight container in the fridge for up to 3 days.

Pesto Hummus
(page 67)

Sweet Potato Hummus
(page 68)

Cilantro Pea Pesto
(page 67)

Pesto Hummus
(page 67)

Sweet Potato Hummus
(page 68)

Cilantro Pea Pesto
(page 67)

BREAKFAST

Early on when I started eating a healthy vegan diet, I was really disappointed that I would have to give up sausage, bacon, and eggs. I became even more disappointed once I realized that pancakes and bagels were also off the menu because their ingredients contained refined wheat and butter or oil. However, I have since learned how to make all these foods in my HV-style approach. My bacon and sausage recipes are very popular on my YouTube cooking show, and many people have said the vegan sausage is the best they have tasted. I also created a tasty recipe for pancakes without the need for wheat flour, oil, eggs, or butter. Here are some great breakfast recipes for you to enjoy!

Quinoa Breakfast Bagels

I've never met someone who didn't like bagels. This bagel recipe is made using quinoa flour, which is high in protein and won't spike your blood sugar like a typical wheat flour bagel would. Toasted or not, these bagels are delicious topped with any of my three cream cheese recipes or when used to make my HV BLT (page 145).

DIFFICULTY
Easy

MAKES
6 bagels

Ingredients

DRY

2½ cups quinoa flour

2 teaspoons baking powder

½ teaspoon baking soda

2 tablespoons date sugar

⅔ teaspoon salt or to taste

2 tablespoons ground flaxseed or ground chia seeds

WET

2½ cups water

1 tablespoon apple cider vinegar

6 tablespoons psyllium husks (see notes)

OPTIONAL TOPPINGS

Sesame seeds

Everything Seasoning

Poppy seeds

Directions

1. Preheat the oven to 350°F. Line a baking sheet with parchment paper and set aside.
2. In a bowl, whisk together all the dry ingredients.
3. In a separate bowl, whisk together the wet ingredients and the psyllium husks. Let rest for 5 minutes until it has a gel-like consistency.
4. Combine the wet and dry ingredients.
5. Wet your hands and divide the dough into 6 equal portions, then roll into balls.
6. On the parchment-lined baking sheet, sprinkle your choice of toppings on areas where you will place your dough balls. Place the dough balls on the toppings.
7. Wet your hands again and flatten and form the dough balls into bagel shapes. Use your finger to create a hole in the center of each one. Generously sprinkle the tops of the bagels with your choice of toppings.
8. Bake for 35 to 40 minutes, or until golden brown. Remove from the oven and allow to cool on a rack completely before cutting.

Notes

Store in an airtight container on the counter for up to 3 days or in the freezer for up to 1 month.

Make sure to use whole psyllium husks for this recipe; using psyllium husk powder will result in a gummy texture. If you find the dough too wet to hold its shape, you may add a couple tablespoons of quinoa flour.

Strawberry Cream Cheese

DIFFICULTY
Easy

MAKES
2 cups

Have you ever tried a bagel smothered with cream cheese and jam? If you have, then you'll enjoy this one as an all-in-one solution. If you haven't, then add it to your list of must-tries—this recipe offers the sweetness of the berries amplified by the dates, without any added refined sugar. You won't be disappointed!

Ingredients

1½ cups raw cashews, soaked for 4–8 hours

¼ cup water

3 tablespoons lemon juice

1 teaspoon apple cider vinegar

¼ teaspoon salt or to taste

2 Medjool dates, pitted

4 large frozen strawberries plus ½ cup coarsely chopped strawberries, divided

Directions

1. Drain the cashews and discard the soaking water.
2. Combine all the ingredients except for the chopped strawberries in a high-speed blender and blend until smooth.
3. Transfer the mixture to a bowl and fold in the chopped strawberries.

Notes

Store in an airtight container in the fridge for up to 3 days.

NUT-FREE: Replace the cashews with raw sunflower seeds.

Garlic and Chives Cream Cheese

DIFFICULTY
Easy

MAKES
2 cups

Who would have thought that whipping up homemade vegan cream cheese could be so easy? Here I've added a healthy dose of roasted garlic and chopped chives to elevate this one to another level. Not only does this pair perfectly with a bagel, but it's also a great addition that will amplify the flavors of any sandwich.

Ingredients

1½ cups raw cashews, soaked for 4–8 hours

½ cup water

3 tablespoons lemon juice

1 teaspoon apple cider vinegar

¼ teaspoon salt or to taste

1 bulb roasted garlic

3 tablespoons chopped chives

Directions

1. Drain the cashews and discard the soaking water.
2. Combine all the ingredients in a high-speed blender except for the chives and blend until smooth.
3. Transfer the mixture to a bowl and fold in the chives.

Notes

Store in an airtight container in the fridge for up to 5 days.

NUT-FREE: Replace the cashews with raw sunflower seeds.

Pomegranate and Cracked Black Pepper Cream Cheese

You may not have considered this unexpected combo of pomegranate and black pepper, but it's a unique twist. The sophisticated flavor pairing and the juicy, pop-in-your-mouth goodness of pomegranate seeds take this cream cheese to the next level. Plus, pomegranates boast an impressive health résumé, besides being packed with nutrients and antioxidants; some studies indicate that they support heart health and digestion among other things. Spread this cream cheese on bagels, crackers, or even fresh fruit and veggies for a bold, nutritious treat!

DIFFICULTY
Easy

MAKES
2 cups

Ingredients

1½ cups raw cashews, soaked for 4–8 hours

½ cup water

3 tablespoons lemon juice

1 teaspoon apple cider vinegar

¼ teaspoon salt or to taste

½ cup pomegranate seeds

¼ teaspoon coarsely ground black pepper

Directions

1. Drain the cashews and discard the soaking water.
2. Combine all the ingredients except for the pomegranate seeds and black pepper in a high-speed blender and blend until smooth.
3. Transfer to a bowl and fold in the pomegranate seeds and black pepper.

Notes

Store in an airtight container in the fridge for up to 3 days.

NUT-FREE: Replace the cashews with raw sunflower seeds.

Notes

Store this loaf in an airtight container for up to 3 days on the counter or slice and freeze in an airtight container for up to 1 month.

Make your own millet flour by grinding the whole millet in a high-speed blender.

Make sure to use whole psyllium husks for this recipe; using psyllium husk powder will result in a gummy texture.

Wheat-Free Cinnamon Raisin Bread

I love cinnamon and raisins—and truthfully, who doesn't love the sweet, warming smell of cinnamon at breakfast? Made with millet flour, which is a more nutrient-dense, lower-glycemic alternative to wheat flour, this lightly sweetened bread has a soft texture and is a healthier alternative to many commercial options.

DIFFICULTY
Medium

MAKES
1 loaf

Ingredients

DRY

2½ cups millet flour (400 grams) (see notes)

2½ teaspoons baking powder (8 grams)

½ teaspoon baking soda (4 grams)

1 tablespoon ground flaxseed or ground chia seeds (7 grams)

⅓ cup finely ground date sugar (40 grams)

1 teaspoon ground cinnamon (3 grams)

¾ teaspoon salt or to taste (5 grams)

1 cup raisins (130 grams)

WET

2½ cups water (600 milliliters)

1 tablespoon apple cider vinegar (16 milliliters)

⅓ cup plus 2 tablespoons whole psyllium husks (40 grams) (see notes)

FILLING

¾ cup date paste (230 grams) (page 43)

1 teaspoon ground cinnamon (3 grams)

Directions

1. Preheat the oven to 350°F. Line a 9 x 5-inch loaf pan with parchment paper and set aside.

2. In a bowl, whisk together the dry ingredients, breaking up any clumps of flour or date sugar.

3. In a separate bowl, whisk together the wet ingredients and the psyllium husks. Let rest for 5 minutes until it has a gel-like consistency.

4. Using a spatula, combine the wet and dry ingredients. The dough will be soft and slightly sticky.

5. Wet your hands and place the dough on a stick-free surface like a piece of parchment paper or a silicone mat. Flatten your dough into a rectangle about 1 inch thick and spread date paste evenly across. Sprinkle on the cinnamon.

6. Using wet hands, carefully roll the dough into a log by lifting one short side of the parchment paper or silicone mat as needed to manipulate the dough. This part can get a little messy, but don't worry: it doesn't have to be perfect.

7. Transfer the log to your prepared loaf pan. With wet hands, smooth the top and tuck the sides of the log as needed. Bake for 80 minutes.

8. Immediately remove the loaf by lifting the edges of the parchment paper and discard the paper. Cool the loaf on a rack completely before cutting.

Mixed Berry Breakfast Bars

Packed with a medley of juicy berries, these delicious and nutritious bars are loaded with health-promoting antioxidants. Berries not only make these bars a tasty breakfast but also help with regulating blood sugar levels. These bars are perfect to have on hand for those busy mornings when you need a quick and healthy breakfast option, or anytime you need a pick-me-up snack.

DIFFICULTY
Medium

MAKES
6 servings

Base and Topping

1¼ cups oat flour

1 cup rolled oats

½ cup mashed very ripe banana

¼ cup date paste (page 43)

¼ cup ground flaxseed

1–2 tablespoons water

2 tablespoons nut butter (see notes)

½ teaspoon ground cinnamon

Pinch of salt

Filling

6 ounces fresh blueberries

6 ounces fresh raspberries

6 ounces fresh blackberries

½ cup date paste (page 43)

½ teaspoon almond or vanilla extract

1 heaping tablespoon arrowroot powder

Directions

1. Preheat the oven to 350°F. Line an 8-inch square baking pan with parchment paper. Set it aside.

2. In a bowl, using a fork, mix the oat flour, oats, banana, date paste, ground flaxseed, water, nut butter, cinnamon, and salt until combined. The mixture will be sticky and crumbly. Set aside.

3. In another bowl, add the berries, date paste, and extract. Mix and coarsely crush the berries with a fork, leaving some whole. Sprinkle the arrowroot over the berry mixture and stir to combine.

4. Prepare the base of the squares. Take half the oat mixture and evenly and firmly press it into the prepared pan.

5. Evenly spread the filling over the top of the base layer.

6. Coarsely crumble and break the remaining half of the oat mixture over the filling.

7. Bake for 25 to 30 minutes, or until the filling is bubbly and the topping is lightly golden.

8. Cool completely in the pan on a rack. Once the mixture has set, lift it out of the pan using the parchment paper. Cut into squares.

Notes

Store in an airtight container in the fridge for up to 3 days or in the freezer for up to 1 month.

Choose nut butter without any added oil or sweetener.

NUT-FREE: Substitute tahini for almond butter.

Nutty Date Granola

Enjoy the wholesome goodness of this oil-free, refined-sugar-free granola, sweetened naturally with dates, of course. This is the perfect healthier replacement for the store-bought stuff. Use it as breakfast cereal or as a crunchy topping for my Golden Mango Breakfast Cup (page 82) or Mixed Berry Breakfast Cup (page 82). Either way, you can't go wrong!

DIFFICULTY
Easy

MAKES
5 cups

Ingredients

12 Medjool dates, pitted

½ cup water

½ cup nut butter (see notes)

1½ teaspoons ground cinnamon

1½ teaspoons vanilla extract

3 cups rolled oats

⅓ cup nuts of choice, coarsely chopped

¼ cup hemp hearts

½ cup pumpkin seeds

2 tablespoons ground flaxseed or ground chia seeds

Notes

Store in an airtight container for up to 1 week.

Choose a nut butter without any added oils or sweetener.

NUT-FREE: Use seed butter of choice and replace chopped nuts with seeds of choice.

Directions

1. Preheat the oven to 325°F. Line a baking sheet with parchment paper.
2. In a high-speed blender, combine the dates, water, and nut butter and blend until smooth. Do not add extra water.
3. In a mixing bowl, combine all the remaining ingredients. Mix to combine.
4. Add the blended date mixture to the dry ingredients and mix to combine.
5. Pour this mixture onto the prepared baking sheet; you'll want to distribute it evenly.
6. Bake for 35 to 40 minutes. Mix at every 7 to 10 minutes for the first 30 minutes. Once the mixture is browning, mix more frequently, at every 5 minutes.
7. Remove the granola from the oven and cool completely. It will crisp up after 30 to 60 minutes.

Mixed Berry Breakfast Cup

DIFFICULTY
Easy

MAKES
2 servings

While berries have a starring role here, they are supported by a nutritious blend of omega-3-rich nuts and seeds. In this recipe, I've paired walnuts, hemp, and chia with whole grain oats and some antioxidant-rich berries. This hearty cup is a thick and satisfying breakfast pudding that will kick-start your day with a burst of flavor and energy.

Ingredients

1 cup walnuts, soaked for at least 2 hours

¼ cup rolled oats

3 tablespoons ground chia seeds

1 teaspoon vanilla extract

½ teaspoon ground cinnamon

3 Medjool dates, pitted

1 cup plant milk

½ cup fresh mixed berries (I like blueberries, strawberries, and blackberries)

OPTIONAL TOPPING

Nutty Date Granola (page 81)

Directions

1. Drain the walnuts and discard the soaking water.
2. Combine all the ingredients except for the berries in a high-speed blender and blend until smooth.
3. Layer the cream mixture and berries as desired. Top with granola, if using, and more berries.

Golden Mango Breakfast Cup

DIFFICULTY
Easy

MAKES
2 servings

Start your day on a golden note with this nutritious and delicious breakfast cup. Not only do the warm and aromatic spices of turmeric, cinnamon, and cardamom add a beautiful flavor to your morning meal, but they are also packed with antioxidants and anti-inflammatory properties, offering a myriad of health benefits in every spoonful.

Ingredients

1 cup walnuts, soaked for at least 2 hours

¼ cup rolled oats

2 tablespoons ground chia seeds

2 tablespoons hemp hearts

1 teaspoon vanilla extract

3 Medjool dates, pitted

½ teaspoon ground turmeric

½ teaspoon ground cinnamon

⅛ teaspoon ground cardamom

Pinch of ground black pepper

1 cup plant milk

Mango, pitted, peeled, and chopped

Directions

1. Drain the walnuts and discard the soaking water.
2. Combine all the ingredients except for the mango in a high-speed blender and blend until smooth.
3. Layer the cream mixture and mango as desired. Top with extra mango.

Notes

Mixed Berry Breakfast Cup	Golden Mango Breakfast Cup
These cups can be made the night before and stored in the fridge. If you don't have berries, sliced apple or stone fruits work well too. Use your favorites to make your own!	These cups can be made the night before and stored in the fridge.

Mushroom Bacon

Made using thinly sliced trumpet mushrooms, this plant-based bacon has a mildly sweet and smoky flavor. My version of this breakfast classic gets its smoky flavor from smoked paprika and a hint of savory saltiness from coconut aminos. Have this mushroom bacon alongside your favorite breakfast foods or use it to build the HV BLT (page 145).

DIFFICULTY
Easy

MAKES
6 servings

Ingredients

24 ounces trumpet mushrooms, sliced lengthwise and thinly (about 1⁄8 inch thick) (see notes)

8 tablespoons coconut aminos

2 teaspoons smoked paprika

1 teaspoon garlic granules

1 teaspoon onion granules

½ teaspoon chipotle seasoning (optional)

Notes

This Mushroom Bacon is best eaten fresh but still makes a delicious addition to a wrap or sandwich the next day. It can be stored in an airtight container in the fridge for up to 3 days.

Can't find trumpet mushrooms? This recipe can also be made using portobello mushrooms.

You can also make your own pumfu (page 23) bacon by cutting pumfu into thin slices and following the same instructions.

Directions

1. Preheat the oven to 375°F. Line a baking sheet with parchment paper.
2. Using a fork, pierce each mushroom slice two to three times.
3. Prepare the marinade by combining the coconut aminos and seasonings in a shallow bowl or pan.
4. Add the sliced mushrooms to the marinade and mix. Let the mushrooms marinate for 3 to 5 minutes.
5. Lay the marinated mushrooms on the prepared baking sheet. Do not overlap them.
6. Bake for 15 minutes, flip and bake for an additional 5 to 10 minutes, or until the edges are crispy. Baking time will vary depending on how large your mushrooms are, how thick you cut them, and how crispy you want them to be.
7. Once your mushrooms are cooked to your liking, remove the pan from the oven and allow them to cool. The mushrooms will crisp up some as they sit, so be careful not to overcook them.

Breakfast Sausage Patties

These mouthwatering patties are seasoned with the classic sausage flavors of sage and fennel—perfect for vegans and nonvegans alike. Add these to a breakfast of pancakes (page 101) or a scramble (page 89) for a complete HV version of an American breakfast, or make a breakfast sandwich with a bagel (page 72) and Pesto Hummus (page 67).

DIFFICULTY
Easy

MAKES
4
patties

Ingredients

2 cups Veggie Sausage Ground (page 33)

2 tablespoons whole psyllium husks (see note)

2 tablespoons arrowroot powder

2 tablespoons chickpea flour

2 teaspoons dried sage

1 teaspoon dried fennel

½ teaspoon dried thyme

½ teaspoon garlic granules

Salt to taste

Directions

1. Preheat the oven to 350°F. Line a baking sheet with parchment paper.
2. In a bowl, combine all the ingredients and mix well.
3. Form into patties and place on the prepared baking sheet.
4. Bake for 10 minutes, flip, and bake for an additional 10 minutes.

Note

These breakfast patties can be baked and stored in the freezer for up to 2 months. Thaw and heat as needed.

No-Egg, Soy-Free Breakfast Scramble

Tofu is often the go-to for vegan scrambles. But if you are looking for a soy-free breakfast option, this scramble is just what you need. Made primarily with pumpkin seeds, it's a great source of zinc, a nutrient that can be challenging to obtain on a plant-based diet. This scramble is soft in texture and gets its eggy flavor from the addition of black salt. A perfect complement to your plant-based morning spread, this dish is delicious, nutritious, and satisfying.

DIFFICULTY
Easy

MAKES
4 servings

Ingredients

1½ cups raw pumpkin seeds, soaked for 6 or more hours

3 cups water

¾ teaspoon ground turmeric

1 teaspoon black salt or to taste (see notes)

1 teaspoon garlic granules (optional)

½ teaspoon onion granules (optional)

Ground black pepper to taste (optional)

Directions

1. Drain and rinse the pumpkin seeds. If you want to reduce the greenish color, you can remove some of the pumpkin seed skins by rubbing and rinsing the seeds.
2. Place the rinsed pumpkin seeds, water, and seasonings in the blender and blend until completely smooth.
3. Heat a skillet on medium. Pour the pumpkin seeds mixture into the pan. Once the mixture starts to bubble and slightly set, after 2 to 3 minutes, begin to gently move it around the pan. Continue this process for another 3 minutes or so, or until the scramble is cooked to your desired consistency. For a dryer scramble, cook longer.

Notes

The pumpkin mixture stores well in the fridge for up to 3 days. If you are preparing the mixture in advance, only add the black salt when you're ready to cook it.

Black salt is also known as *kala namak* and is often used in Indian cooking. It provides this pumpkin scramble with an eggy flavor. Black salt can be found at Indian grocery stores or online.

On-the-Go Frittatas

The ultimate solution for a quick and convenient breakfast on the go, these breakfast frittatas can be easily prepped ahead of time and stored in the fridge for up to five days. Simply pop them in the toaster oven to warm them up before heading out to start your day. With protein-rich chickpea flour and pumpkin seeds, these frittatas are a great way to enjoy a hassle-free breakfast that's both satisfying and time-saving.

DIFFICULTY
Easy

MAKES
12 muffin portions

Ingredients

- 1 cup pumpkin seeds, soaked for 6 or more hours
- ¾ cup chickpea flour
- 2 cups water
- 1 teaspoon garlic granules
- 1½ teaspoons black salt (see notes)
- ¾ teaspoon ground turmeric
- ½ teaspoon smoked paprika
- ¼ teaspoon ground black pepper
- ½ teaspoon baking powder
- 1 teaspoon lemon juice
- ¾ cup minced red pepper
- ½ cup chopped green onions
- Chopped green onions, for garnish (optional)

Directions

1. Preheat the oven to 325°F. Line a muffin tin with parchment liners and set aside.
2. Drain the pumpkin seeds and discard the soaking water.
3. Place all the ingredients, except the red pepper and green onions, in a blender. Blend into a smooth batter.
4. Add the red pepper and green onions to the batter and mix with a spoon until just combined.
5. Fill each muffin cup using ¼ cup of the mixture and top with additional green onions, if using.
6. Bake for 20 to 25 minutes, or until golden in color. Cool for 10 minutes before removing from the pan.

Notes

Store in an airtight container in the fridge for up to 5 days.

You can prep the batter in advance, but only add the black salt, baking powder, and veggies when you're ready to bake them.

Black salt is also known as *kala namak* and is often used in Indian cooking. It provides an eggy flavor. Black salt can be found at Indian grocery stores or online.

Notes

Mango-Coconut Chia Pudding

I use full-fat coconut milk that doesn't contain any thickeners or stabilizers. This can be found in a can or tetra pack at many health-food stores and online.

If you don't have or don't like mango, you can swap in other fruits: try pineapple for a tropical flare, melon, stone fruits, or berries, all of which taste great with coconut.

Cherry Chia Pudding

This can be prepared up to one day in advance and kept in the refrigerator until ready to serve. Cherries may oxidize slightly if made in advance.

Mango-Coconut Chia Pudding

DIFFICULTY
Easy

MAKES
2 servings

I came up with this creation inspired by the tropical flavors of Thai mango sticky rice. Rather than sticky rice, we're using chia seeds, which are a good source of plant protein and are rich in antioxidants, minerals, and omega-3 fatty acids. This recipe is so delicious, it could easily be in the dessert section, so get ready to indulge with each spoonful.

Ingredients

1½ cups coconut milk (see notes)

⅓ cup date paste (page 43)

6 tablespoons chia seeds

1 fresh mango, peeled, pitted, and diced, divided (see notes)

Toasted coconut, for garnish (optional)

Directions

① In a bowl, whisk together the coconut milk and date paste until combined.

② Add the chia seeds and mix thoroughly.

③ Pour the mixture equally into 2 cups or small bowls. Drop half the diced mango into the cups.

④ Allow to set in the fridge for a minimum of 1 hour, or until set.

⑤ Top with extra mango and toasted coconut, if using. These cups can be prepared up to 1 day in advance and kept in the refrigerator until ready to serve.

Cherry Chia Pudding

DIFFICULTY
Easy

MAKES
1 serving

This vibrant and nutritious pudding can start or end your day! Containing potassium and polyphenols, both of which are good for the heart, cherries also bring a sweet and tangy flavor to this treat. Chia seeds, known for their impressive anti-inflammatory properties, give this pudding its creamy texture. This pudding is not only a delicious choice but is also a nourishing one for your overall well-being. The recipe makes a single serving, but you can double it as needed.

Ingredients

1 cup fresh or frozen dark sweet cherries, pitted, divided

½ cup plant milk

2 Medjool dates, pitted

3 tablespoons chia seeds

Fresh cherries for topping (optional)

Directions

① Combine ½ cup of the cherries, the plant milk, and dates in a high-speed blender and blend until smooth.

② Add the chia seeds and blend thoroughly.

③ Mix in the remaining ½ cup of cherries. Pour into a serving cup and refrigerate for 1 or more hours. Garnish with fresh cherries, if using.

Strawberry Cheesecake Baked Oats

Oats are a common breakfast food, with good reason: They are nutritious, high in fiber, help lower cholesterol, and more. But let's face it: Oatmeal can be boring. With a cream cheese topping and strawberry sauce, these strawberry baked oats are the ultimate breakfast upgrade! Sometimes you want a little something extra to start your day; with a boost of protein from the nut butter, this breakfast is both decadent and nutritious.

DIFFICULTY
Easy

MAKES
6 servings

Ingredients

OAT BASE

2 cups rolled oats

2 tablespoons ground flaxseed or ground chia seeds

1 teaspoon ground cinnamon

Pinch of salt (optional)

1¼ cups plant milk

1 cup date paste (page 43)

1½ teaspoons vanilla extract

¼ cup nut or seed butter (see notes)

2 cups chopped fresh strawberries

CREAM CHEESE TOPPING

¾ cup raw cashews, soaked for 4–8 hours

¼–½ cup plant milk

2–3 Medjool dates, pitted

2 teaspoons lemon juice

STRAWBERRY SAUCE

2 cups frozen strawberries

Directions

OAT BASE

1. Preheat the oven to 375°F. Line an 8-inch or 9-inch pan with parchment paper.
2. In a bowl, combine the rolled oats, ground flaxseed, cinnamon, and salt, if using. Set aside.
3. Blend the plant milk, date paste, vanilla extract, and nut butter until smooth.
4. Combine the wet and dry ingredients.
5. Mix in the strawberries and pour the batter into the prepared pan.
6. Bake the oat mixture for 30 minutes or until slightly firm to the touch.

CREAM CHEESE TOPPING

1. Drain the cashews and discard the soaking water.
2. Combine all the ingredients in a high-speed blender and blend until smooth.

STRAWBERRY SAUCE

1. Add the strawberries to a small saucepan and simmer on low for about 30 minutes, or until the strawberries break down and thicken.
2. Allow to cool and then blend in a high-speed blender until smooth.

Once all the components are ready, drizzle the cream cheese topping and strawberry sauce over the whole pan or top the individual servings.

Notes

Oats can be stored in the fridge in an airtight container for up to 3 days.

Choose a nut butter without any added oils or sweetener.

Peanut Butter, Banana, and Chocolate Chip Baked Oats

Who doesn't like cake for breakfast? These blended baked oats cook up just like a cake, making them a fun and delicious breakfast option for the whole family. Whether baked in a cake pan for sharing, or in single-size portions for a convenient grab-and-go meal, these baked oats are the perfect mix of hearty, healthy, and delicious.

DIFFICULTY
Easy

MAKES
6-inch pan or four 4-inch ramekins

Ingredients

- 1 cup rolled oats
- 1 ripe banana
- ½ cup plant milk
- ¼ cup peanut butter (see notes)
- 3 medjool dates, pitted
- ½ teaspoon vanilla extract
- ½ teaspoon ground cinnamon
- ½ teaspoon baking powder
- ½ cup date-sweetened chocolate chips

Directions

1. Preheat the oven to 350°F. Line a 6-inch square pan with parchment paper.
2. Combine all the ingredients except for the chocolate chips in a high-speed blender and blend until smooth.
3. Transfer the mixture to a bowl and fold in the chocolate chips.
4. Add the batter to the prepared pan. Bake for 25 to 30 minutes, or until firm to the touch.

Notes

Oats can be stored in the fridge in an airtight container for up to 3 days.

Choose a peanut butter without any added oil or sugar.

This can also be made in individual-size ramekins. If you're using ramekins, reduce the baking time by 3 to 5 minutes.

Carrot Cake Overnight Oats and Chocolate-Strawberry Overnight Oats

Whether you're craving the cozy flavor of carrot cake or the classic combo of strawberries and chocolate, overnight oats make for a convenient, healthy breakfast. Mix them up the night before or prep a batch for a few days—either way, you can't go wrong.

DIFFICULTY
Easy

MAKES
2 servings

Ingredients

CARROT CAKE OVERNIGHT OATS

1½ cups plant milk
6 tablespoons date paste (page 43)
1½ cups rolled oats
½ teaspoon ground cinnamon
½ teaspoon minced fresh ginger, or ⅛ teaspoon ground ginger
¼ teaspoon ground turmeric
⅛ teaspoon ground black pepper
Pinch of cloves
Pinch of salt
⅔ cup grated carrots
¼ cup raisins (optional)
⅓ cup chopped walnuts (optional)

CHOCOLATE-STRAWBERRY OVERNIGHT OATS

2 cups plant milk
1 teaspoon vanilla extract
6 tablespoons date paste (page 43)
2 cups rolled oats
2 tablespoons cocoa powder
⅔ cup chopped strawberries

Directions

1. Place the plant milk and date paste in your cup or bowl and mix to combine.
2. Add the oats and the remaining ingredients and mix again.
3. Divide into two separate cups or bowls.
4. Cover and refrigerate for a minimum of 2 hours. The longer the bowls sit, the thicker the oats will be.

Notes

Oats can be stored in the fridge in an airtight container for up to 3 days.

Enjoy these oats cold or warmed up.

HV Simple Pancakes

I love pancakes for breakfast, but I don't love using traditional high-glycemic flour. Swapping in oat and almond flour creates a healthier alternative: one that is nutty, flavorful, and versatile. It serves as the perfect foundation for a range of pancake variations. Whether you prefer blueberries or chocolate chips, this is a must-have recipe to add to your breakfast rotation.

DIFFICULTY
Easy

MAKES
2–4 pancakes

Ingredients

½ cup puréed overripe banana

½–¾ cup plant milk

1½ teaspoons vanilla extract

½ cup oat flour

½ cup almond flour

1 tablespoon ground flaxseed or ground chia seeds

2 teaspoons baking powder

¾ teaspoon ground cinnamon

Pinch of salt (optional)

OPTIONAL TOPPINGS

Fresh or frozen berries (see note)

Date paste (page 43)

Berry sauce (pages 94 and 255)

Directions

1. In a bowl, combine the banana purée, ½ cup of the plant milk, and vanilla extract. Whisk to combine.

2. In a separate bowl, combine the oat flour, almond flour, ground flaxseed, baking powder, ground cinnamon, and salt, if using.

3. Add the wet ingredients to the dry ingredients. Mix to combine. Use the remaining ¼ cup of the plant milk if necessary to create a thick but pourable consistency. Batter will thicken as it sits.

4. Heat a skillet on medium-low. Pour the pancake batter into desired size pancake. Cook for 2 to 4 minutes, or until the pancake is cooked halfway with some bubbles on top. Flip and cook for an additional 2 to 4 minutes. Enjoy these pancakes topped with fresh berries, date paste, or a generous pour of berry sauce.

Note

If adding frozen berries, make sure to drain excess juice.

Lemon-Blueberry Breakfast Cookies (page 103)

Strawberry–Chocolate Chip Breakfast Cookies (page 104)

Lemon-Blueberry Breakfast Cookies

If you love the flavor combination of lemon and blueberry like I do, then you'll love these! Although all berries are super healthy, blueberries may just be my favorite. They are one of the fruits highest in antioxidants, which are responsible for protecting our cells from daily damage and therefore help our bodies stave off disease. Whether you're looking for a convenient and tasty snack, or you want to boost your antioxidant intake, these breakfast cookies are a great and satisfying option. They're also great for breakfast on the go.

DIFFICULTY
Easy

MAKES
12 cookies

Ingredients

2 tablespoons ground flaxseed plus 5 tablespoons water (flax egg)

2 cups rolled oats

½ cup almond flour

¾ teaspoon baking soda

1 tablespoon poppy seeds

½ teaspoon ground turmeric

⅛ teaspoon ground black pepper

1 tablespoon lemon zest

½ cup nut butter (see notes)

1 cup date paste (page 43)

1 teaspoon vanilla extract

2 teaspoons lemon juice

1 pint fresh or frozen blueberries (see notes)

Notes

Store in an airtight container in the fridge for up to 5 days.

Choose a nut butter without any added oil or sugar.

If using frozen blueberries, thaw and drain excess liquid before adding them.

Directions

1. Preheat the oven to 350°F. Line a baking sheet with parchment paper.
2. Combine the ground flaxseed and water and set aside for 5 to 10 minutes.
3. In a bowl, add the rolled oats, almond flour, baking soda, poppy seeds, turmeric, black pepper, and lemon zest and mix to combine.
4. In a separate bowl, combine the nut butter, date paste, vanilla extract, and lemon juice. Add previously made flax egg and mix.
5. Add the dry mixture to the wet mixture and mix to combine. Fold in the fresh blueberries.
6. Use a 2- to 3-tablespoon cookie scoop to scoop and shape 12 cookies onto the baking sheet 2 inches apart. Bake for 18 to 22 minutes. Allow the cookies to cool for 10 minutes before eating.

Strawberry–Chocolate Chip Breakfast Cookies

There's no doubt that strawberries and dark chocolate make a delicious pair, but they're also a powerhouse combo of antioxidants, vitamins, and flavonoids. Add a dash of cinnamon, known for its blood-sugar-regulating and anti-inflammatory properties, and mix in some fiber-rich oats, and you've got breakfast cookies that are as nourishing as they are satisfying.

DIFFICULTY
Easy

MAKES
12 cookies

Ingredients

2 tablespoons ground flaxseed plus 5 tablespoons water (flax egg)

2 cups rolled oats

½ cup almond flour

¾ teaspoon baking soda

¾ teaspoon ground cinnamon

½ cup nut butter (see notes)

1 cup date paste (page 43)

1 teaspoon vanilla extract

2 teaspoons lemon juice

1½ cups chopped strawberries

½ cup date-sweetened chocolate chips

Notes

Store in an airtight container in the fridge for up to 5 days.

Choose a nut butter without any added oil or sugar.

Directions

① Preheat the oven to 350°F. Line a baking sheet with parchment paper.

② Combine the ground flaxseed and water and set aside for 5 to 10 minutes.

③ In a bowl, add the rolled oats, almond flour, baking soda, and ground cinnamon and mix to combine.

④ In a separate bowl, add the nut butter, date paste, vanilla extract, and lemon juice and mix to combine. Add previously made flax egg and mix.

⑤ Add the dry mixture to the wet mixture and mix to combine. Fold in the strawberries and chocolate chips.

⑥ Use a 2- to 3-tablespoon cookie scoop to scoop and shape 12 cookies onto the baking sheet 2 inches apart. Bake for 18 to 22 minutes. Allow the cookies to cool for 10 minutes before eating.

Golden Breakfast Cookies

While golden milk became popular in the West a few years ago, it is actually a traditional Ayurvedic drink. The warming addition of ginger, turmeric, cinnamon, and cardamom are not only filled with health-promoting benefits; they are also tasty. Adding them to a breakfast cookie is an easy way to incorporate their benefits into your daily routine!

DIFFICULTY
Easy

MAKES
12 cookies

Ingredients

2 tablespoons ground flaxseed plus 5 tablespoons water (flax egg)

2 cups rolled oats

½ cup almond flour

¾ teaspoon baking soda

1 teaspoon ground cinnamon

1 teaspoon fresh ginger

1 teaspoon ground turmeric

½ teaspoon ground cardamom

⅛ teaspoon ground black pepper

½ cup nut butter (see notes)

1 cup date paste (page 43)

1 teaspoon vanilla extract

2 teaspoons lemon juice

½ cup chopped pistachios (see notes)

Notes

Store in an airtight container in the fridge for up to 5 days

Choose a nut butter without any added oil or sugar.

Swap any nut or seed of choice for the pistachios in this recipe.

Directions

① Preheat the oven to 350°F. Line a baking sheet with parchment paper.

② Combine the ground flaxseed and water and set aside for 5 to 10 minutes.

③ In a bowl, add the rolled oats, almond flour, baking soda, cinnamon, ginger, turmeric, cardamom, and black pepper and mix to combine.

④ In a separate bowl, add the nut butter, date paste, vanilla extract, and lemon juice and mix to combine. Add previously made flax egg and mix.

⑤ Add the dry mixture to the wet mixture and mix to combine. Fold in the pistachios.

⑥ Use a 2- to 3-tablespoon cookie scoop to scoop and shape 12 cookies onto the baking sheet 2 inches apart. Bake for 18 to 22 minutes. Allow the cookies to cool for 10 minutes before eating.

Carrot Cake Breakfast Cookies

I never miss a chance to work antimicrobial, anti-inflammatory, and antioxidant-rich spices like ginger, cinnamon, and cloves into a recipe. Carrot cake is already known for a warming blend of those exact spices, so taking those flavors and molding them into cookies? It's the perfect way to get those health benefits while enjoying everything we love about carrot cake—only, we're having it for breakfast!

DIFFICULTY
Easy

MAKES
12 cookies

Ingredients

2 tablespoons ground flaxseed plus 5 tablespoons water (flax egg)

2 cups rolled oats

½ cup almond flour

1½ teaspoons ground cinnamon

½ teaspoon ground ginger

⅛ teaspoon ground cloves

¾ teaspoon baking soda

1 cup grated carrot

½ cup nut butter (see notes)

1 cup date paste (page 43)

1 teaspoon vanilla extract

2 teaspoons lemon juice

½ cup chopped walnuts or pecans

½ cup raisins

Notes

Store in an airtight container in the fridge for up to 5 days.

Choose a nut butter without any added oil or sugar.

Directions

1. Preheat the oven to 350°F. Line a baking sheet with parchment paper.
2. Combine the ground flaxseed and water and set aside for 5 to 10 minutes.
3. In a bowl, add the rolled oats, almond flour, ground cinnamon, ground ginger, ground cloves, and baking soda and mix to combine.
4. In a separate bowl, add the carrot, nut butter, date paste, vanilla extract, and lemon juice and mix to combine. Add previously made flax egg and mix.
5. Add the dry mixture to the wet mixture and mix to combine. Fold in the nuts and raisins.
6. Use a 2- to 3-tablespoon cookie scoop to scoop and shape 12 cookies onto the baking sheet 2 inches apart. Bake for 18 to 22 minutes. Allow the cookies to cool for 10 minutes before eating.

Golden
Breakfast
Cookies
(page 105)
Carrot Cake
Breakfast Cookies
(page 106)

HIGH-PROTEIN SNACKS

Many people who follow a plant-based diet are concerned about whether they're getting enough protein. When consuming a diverse diet of beans and legumes, whole grains, fruits, vegetables, and nuts and seeds, getting enough protein is typically not an issue. However, if you want to up your protein intake, I have included some plant-based protein bars and drinks that are easy to prepare and grab on the go. Here, you will find both protein shakes and bars that contain 18 to 20 grams of protein per serving (see recipe notes).

Peanut Butter, Chocolate Chip Protein Bars

Commercial bars tout their high-protein content, but the fine print is often full of fillers, additives, and chemicals. I'm also going to tout the high-protein content in these bars, but there's no fine print here: The addition of ground flaxseed and chia seeds adds even more protein, as well as key nutrients, including omega-3 fatty acids and antioxidants. These chewy, chocolatey protein bars are a perfect on-the-go snack that will keep you feeling satisfied any time of day!

DIFFICULTY
Easy

MAKES
8 bars

Ingredients

½ cup peanut butter (see notes)

¼ cup plant milk

1 teaspoon vanilla extract

8 Medjool dates, pitted

1½ cups rolled oats

½ cup unsweetened, unflavored plant-based protein powder

¼ cup ground flaxseed

¼ cup ground chia seeds

¼ teaspoon salt (optional)

½ cup date-sweetened chocolate chips

Directions

1. Line an 8-inch pan with parchment paper.
2. In a food processor, combine the peanut butter, plant milk, and vanilla extract. Add the dates and process until smooth.
3. Add the rolled oats, protein powder, ground flaxseed, ground chia, and salt, if using. Process until combined and a very thick dough is formed. If the dough is too moist, add some more protein. If the dough is too dry, add small amounts of plant milk.
4. Fold in the chocolate chips. You can do this directly in the food processor or transfer the mixture to a bowl.
5. Press the mixture into the prepared pan. Place in the freezer for 1 hour. Cut into 8 equal pieces.

Notes

Store in an airtight container for up to 1 week or in the freezer for up to 1 month.

Choose a peanut butter without any added oil or sugar.

Any nut butter of choice can be used to replace the peanut butter if you cannot have peanuts.

PROTEIN POWDER: The total grams of protein here will depend on your powder of choice. I recommend choosing a brand of organic, unflavored plant-based protein powder. Most brands contain between 45 and 48 grams of protein per ½ cup, which makes these 20 grams per bar. Your choice of nut butter and plant milk may also amp up the protein.

Peanut Butter, Chocolate Chip Protein Bars (page 110)

Double-Chocolate Protein Bars (page 112)

Double-Chocolate Protein Bars

Calling all chocolate lovers! Chocolate chips plus cocoa powder amp up the flavor here, which makes these the perfect fix. These do double duty if you are craving something sweet but are trying to cut back. The best of both worlds!

DIFFICULTY
Easy

MAKES
8 bars

Ingredients

- ½ cup nut or seed butter (see notes)
- ¼ cup plant milk
- 1 teaspoon vanilla extract
- 8 Medjool dates, pitted
- 1½ cups rolled oats
- ½ cup unsweetened plant-based protein powder
- ¼ cup ground flaxseed
- ¼ cup ground chia seeds
- ¼ cup cocoa powder
- ¼ teaspoon salt (optional)
- ½ cup date-sweetened chocolate chips

Directions

1. Line an 8-inch pan with parchment paper.
2. In a food processor, combine the nut butter, plant milk, and vanilla extract. Add the dates and process until smooth.
3. Add the rolled oats, protein powder, ground flaxseed, ground chia, cocoa powder, and salt, if using. Process until combined and a very thick dough is formed. If the dough is too moist, add some more protein. If the dough is too dry, add very small amounts of plant milk.
4. Fold in the chocolate chips. You can do this directly in the food processor or transfer the mixture to a bowl.
5. Press the mixture into the prepared pan. Place in the freezer for 1 hour. Cut into 6 to 8 equal pieces.

Notes

Store in an airtight container for up to 1 week or in the freezer for up to 1 month.

Choose a nut butter without any added oils or sweetener.

NUT-FREE: Replace the nut butter with seed butter.

PROTEIN POWDER: The total grams of protein here will depend on your powder of choice. I recommend choosing a brand of organic, unflavored plant-based protein powder. Most brands contain between 45 and 48 grams of protein per ½ cup, which makes these 20 grams per bar. Your choice of nut butter and plant milk may also amp up the protein.

Peanut Butter, Chocolate Chip Protein Bars (page 110)

Double-Chocolate Protein Bars (page 112)

Double-Chocolate Protein Bars

Calling all chocolate lovers! Chocolate chips plus cocoa powder amp up the flavor here, which makes these the perfect fix. These do double duty if you are craving something sweet but are trying to cut back. The best of both worlds!

DIFFICULTY
Easy

MAKES
8 bars

Ingredients

½ cup nut or seed butter (see notes)

¼ cup plant milk

1 teaspoon vanilla extract

8 Medjool dates, pitted

1½ cups rolled oats

½ cup unsweetened plant-based protein powder

¼ cup ground flaxseed

¼ cup ground chia seeds

¼ cup cocoa powder

¼ teaspoon salt (optional)

½ cup date-sweetened chocolate chips

Directions

(1) Line an 8-inch pan with parchment paper.

(2) In a food processor, combine the nut butter, plant milk, and vanilla extract. Add the dates and process until smooth.

(3) Add the rolled oats, protein powder, ground flaxseed, ground chia, cocoa powder, and salt, if using. Process until combined and a very thick dough is formed. If the dough is too moist, add some more protein. If the dough is too dry, add very small amounts of plant milk.

(4) Fold in the chocolate chips. You can do this directly in the food processor or transfer the mixture to a bowl.

(5) Press the mixture into the prepared pan. Place in the freezer for 1 hour. Cut into 6 to 8 equal pieces.

Notes

Store in an airtight container for up to 1 week or in the freezer for up to 1 month.

Choose a nut butter without any added oils or sweetener.

NUT-FREE: Replace the nut butter with seed butter.

PROTEIN POWDER: The total grams of protein here will depend on your powder of choice. I recommend choosing a brand of organic, unflavored plant-based protein powder. Most brands contain between 45 and 48 grams of protein per ½ cup, which makes these 20 grams per bar. Your choice of nut butter and plant milk may also amp up the protein.

Cinnamon-Fig Protein Bars

Store-bought protein bars may seem like a healthy option, but most commercial brands have unhealthy ingredients. These bars have all the flavor and none of the processed ingredients and are a protein bomb to boot. Figs give you that extra protein but also add iron, potassium, magnesium, and calcium, all of which are important for maintaining optimal health!

DIFFICULTY
Easy

MAKES
8 bars

Ingredients

½ cup nut or seed butter (see notes)

¼ cup plus 2 tablespoons plant milk

1 teaspoon vanilla extract

6 Medjool dates, pitted

2 figs plus ½ cup chopped figs, divided

1½ cups rolled oats

½ cup unsweetened plant-based protein powder

¼ cup ground flaxseed

¼ cup ground chia seeds

1 teaspoon ground cinnamon

¼ teaspoon salt (optional)

Directions

1. Line an 8-inch pan with parchment paper.
2. In a food processor, combine the nut butter, plant milk, and vanilla extract. Add the dates and 2 figs and process until smooth.
3. Add the rolled oats, protein powder, ground flaxseed, ground chia, ground cinnamon, and salt, if using. Process until combined and a very thick dough is formed. If the dough is too moist, add some more protein powder. If the dough is too dry, add very small amounts of plant milk.
4. Fold in the chopped figs.
5. Press the mixture into the prepared pan. Place in the freezer for 1 hour. Cut into 8 equal pieces.

Notes

Store in an airtight container for up to 1 week or in the freezer for up to 1 month.

Choose a nut butter without any added oils or sweetener.

NUT-FREE: Replace the nut butter with seed butter.

PROTEIN POWDER: The total grams of protein here will depend on your powder of choice. I recommend choosing a brand of organic, unflavored plant-based protein powder. Most brands contain between 45 and 48 grams of protein per ½ cup, which makes these 20 grams per bar. Your choice of nut butter and plant milk may also amp up the protein.

Cinnamon-Fig Protein Bars (page 113)

Strawberry Shortcake Protein Bars (page 115)

Cinnamon-Fig Protein Bars

Store-bought protein bars may seem like a healthy option, but most commercial brands have unhealthy ingredients. These bars have all the flavor and none of the processed ingredients and are a protein bomb to boot. Figs give you that extra protein but also add iron, potassium, magnesium, and calcium, all of which are important for maintaining optimal health!

DIFFICULTY
Easy

MAKES
8 bars

Ingredients

½ cup nut or seed butter (see notes)

¼ cup plus 2 tablespoons plant milk

1 teaspoon vanilla extract

6 Medjool dates, pitted

2 figs plus ½ cup chopped figs, divided

1½ cups rolled oats

½ cup unsweetened plant-based protein powder

¼ cup ground flaxseed

¼ cup ground chia seeds

1 teaspoon ground cinnamon

¼ teaspoon salt (optional)

Directions

1. Line an 8-inch pan with parchment paper.
2. In a food processor, combine the nut butter, plant milk, and vanilla extract. Add the dates and 2 figs and process until smooth.
3. Add the rolled oats, protein powder, ground flaxseed, ground chia, ground cinnamon, and salt, if using. Process until combined and a very thick dough is formed. If the dough is too moist, add some more protein powder. If the dough is too dry, add very small amounts of plant milk.
4. Fold in the chopped figs.
5. Press the mixture into the prepared pan. Place in the freezer for 1 hour. Cut into 8 equal pieces.

Notes

Store in an airtight container for up to 1 week or in the freezer for up to 1 month.

Choose a nut butter without any added oils or sweetener.

NUT-FREE: Replace the nut butter with seed butter.

PROTEIN POWDER: The total grams of protein here will depend on your powder of choice. I recommend choosing a brand of organic, unflavored plant-based protein powder. Most brands contain between 45 and 48 grams of protein per ½ cup, which makes these 20 grams per bar. Your choice of nut butter and plant milk may also amp up the protein.

Cinnamon-Fig
Protein Bars
(page 113)
Strawberry
Shortcake
Protein Bars
(page 115)

Strawberry Shortcake Protein Bars

Store-bought protein bars are often filled with refined sugars, oil, and artificial flavors. Once you see how easy it is to make your own, you'll never go back to store-bought again. If you're a fruit lover, feel free to swap the freeze-dried strawberries for freeze-dried blueberries or cherries to add even more variety!

DIFFICULTY
Easy

MAKES
8 bars

Ingredients

½ cup nut or seed butter (see notes)

¼ cup plant milk

2 teaspoons vanilla extract

8 Medjool dates, pitted

1½ cups rolled oats

½ cup unsweetened plant-based protein powder

¼ cup ground flaxseed

¼ cup ground chia seeds

¼ teaspoon salt (optional)

2 cups freeze-dried strawberries (see notes)

Directions

1. Line an 8-inch pan with parchment paper.
2. In a food processor, combine the nut butter, plant milk, and vanilla extract. Add the dates and process until smooth.
3. Add the rolled oats, protein powder, ground flaxseed, ground chia, and salt, if using. Process until combined and a very thick dough is formed. If the dough is too moist, add some more protein powder. If the dough is too dry, add very small amounts of plant milk.
4. Fold in the strawberries.
5. Press the mixture into the prepared pan. Place in the freezer for 1 hour. Cut into 8 equal pieces.

Notes

Store in an airtight container for up to 1 week or in the freezer for up to 1 month.

Choose a nut butter without any added oils or sweetener.

FRUIT SWAPS: Try freeze-dried blueberries or cherries.

NUT-FREE: Replace the nut butter with seed butter.

PROTEIN POWDER: The total grams of protein here will depend on your powder of choice. I recommend choosing a brand of organic, unflavored plant-based protein powder. Most brands contain between 45 and 48 grams of protein per ½ cup, which makes these 20 grams per bar. Your choice of nut butter and plant milk may also amp up the protein.

Protein Shakes

Introducing five whole food plant-based protein shakes. These shakes get the bulk of their protein from hemp, chia, and flaxseed. In addition to being high in protein and omega-3 fatty acids, each of these seeds has its own unique benefits, from supporting cardiovascular health to improving digestion and helping to regulate blood sugar.

Whether you love chocolate, the refreshing flavor of key lime, or the tropical flavors of mango and pineapple, these protein drinks are a great meal on-the-go or post-workout replenisher. Try them all and elevate your protein shake game!

KEY LIME AND COCONUT PROTEIN SHAKE

DIFFICULTY
Easy

MAKES
1 drink

Ingredients

¼ cup coconut milk (see notes)

½ cup plant milk

5 tablespoons hemp hearts (see notes)

5 teaspoons ground chia seeds (see notes)

½ teaspoon vanilla extract

1 teaspoon key lime zest (see notes)

Squeeze of key lime juice

4 Medjool dates, pitted, or to taste

1 cup ice

Directions

Place all the ingredients in a blender and blend until smooth.

Notes

Look for full-fat coconut milk that doesn't contain any stabilizers or thickeners.

Replace the hemp and chia seeds with 1 serving of your favorite unflavored plant-based protein powder.

If you can't find key limes in your area, regular limes will work.

PROTEIN: 23 grams.

(recipes continue)

Chocolate Protein Shake (page 119)

Key Lime and Coconut Protein Shake (page 116)

Strawberry
Protein Shake
(page 120)
Piña Colada
Protein Shake
(page 119)
Mango
Protein Shake
(page 120)

CHOCOLATE PROTEIN SHAKE

DIFFICULTY
Easy

MAKES
1 drink

Ingredients

3 tablespoons unsweetened cocoa powder

¼ avocado

3 tablespoons hemp hearts (see notes)

2 teaspoons ground chia seeds (see notes)

1 tablespoon nut or seed butter (see notes)

2–4 Medjool dates, pitted

1 cup plant milk

½–1 cup ice (optional)

Directions

Place all the ingredients in a blender and blend until smooth.

Notes

Replace the hemp and chia seeds with 1 serving of your favorite unflavored plant-based protein powder.

Choose a nut butter without any added oils or sweetener.

PROTEIN: 23 grams.

PIÑA COLADA PROTEIN SHAKE

DIFFICULTY
Easy

MAKES
1 drink

Ingredients

2 cups frozen pineapple chunks

½ cup coconut milk (see notes)

½ cup plant milk

4 tablespoons hemp hearts (see notes)

4 teaspoons ground chia seeds (see notes)

Directions

Place all the ingredients in a blender and blend until smooth.

Notes

Look for full-fat coconut milk that doesn't contain any stabilizers or thickeners.

Replace the hemp and chia seeds with your favorite unflavored plant-based protein powder.

PROTEIN: 20 grams.

(recipes continue)

STRAWBERRY PROTEIN SHAKE

DIFFICULTY
Easy

MAKES
1 drink

Ingredients

1 cup frozen strawberries

½ teaspoon vanilla extract

4 tablespoons hemp hearts (see notes)

2 teaspoons ground golden flaxseed (see notes)

3 teaspoons ground chia seeds (see notes)

2 Medjool dates, pitted

1 cup plant milk

Directions

Place all the ingredients in a blender and blend until smooth.

Notes

Replace the hemp, flaxseed, and chia seeds with your unflavored plant-based protein of choice.

PROTEIN: 19 grams.

MANGO PROTEIN SHAKE

DIFFICULTY
Easy

MAKES
1 drink

Ingredients

1 cup chopped frozen mango

½ teaspoon vanilla extract

4 tablespoons hemp hearts (see notes)

2 teaspoons ground golden flaxseed (see notes)

3 teaspoons ground chia seeds (see notes)

1–2 Medjool dates, pitted

1 cup plant milk

Directions

Place all the ingredients in a blender and blend until smooth.

Notes

Replace the hemp, flaxseed, and chia seeds with your unflavored plant-based protein of choice.

PROTEIN: 19 grams.

DRINKS

Whether you're craving a cool, refreshing beverage to beat the summer heat or a warm, comforting drink to cozy up with during the fall and winter, you'll find something here to satisfy your taste buds year-round. Best of all, every recipe is naturally sweetened with fruit—no refined sugar needed!

Pear-Mint-Lime Refresher

DIFFICULTY
Easy

MAKES
1 serving

Pears are high in fiber, potassium, and vitamin K. Now that may not sound like an exciting base for a drink, but blend pears with mint and lime, and you have a slushy refresher that tastes like a spring day and is replenishing. Note: This recipe calls for frozen pears; I recommend coring and chopping your pears and then freezing them. Keep some on hand whenever you want a vibrant pick-me-up.

Ingredients

2 frozen ripe pears, cored and peeled

1/4 lime, peeled

1/4 cup packed fresh mint

1/2–3/4 cup plant milk

Slice of lime and sprig of mint, for garnish

Directions

1. Combine all the ingredients in a high-speed blender and blend until smooth.
2. Garnish with a slice of lime and sprig of mint.

Watermelon-Mint-Lime Refresher

DIFFICULTY
Easy

MAKES
1 serving

Super hydrating, not to mention flavorful, watermelon is truly refreshing. Mint can help improve digestion. Pair these two with lime, and you have another option for summer in a glass. Note: This recipe calls for frozen watermelon; I recommend chopping the melon or using a melon baller to scoop the fruit and then freezing the melon.

Ingredients

2 heaping cups frozen watermelon

1/4 lime, peeled

1/4 cup packed fresh mint

1/2–3/4 cup plant milk

Slice of lime and sprig of mint, for garnish

Directions

1. Combine all the ingredients in a high-speed blender and blend until smooth.
2. Garnish with a slice of lime and sprig of mint.

Blueberry Lemonade
(page 127)

Strawberry Lemonade
(page 128)

Blueberry Lemonade

You may know that studies suggest blueberries may help lower blood sugar and have many health benefits; they also can provide a refreshing base for this alternative to traditional lemonade. The natural sweetness of the berries and apples means you don't need to add any refined sugar. You'll still get that classic tang while indulging in healthier ingredients. Note that you can use a juicer or a blender here; I've provided instructions for both methods below.

DIFFICULTY
Easy

MAKES
2 servings

Ingredients

1 pint fresh blueberries

2 apples, cored and cut (see notes)

1 lemon, peeled

Notes

If you're using the blender method, peel your apples first.

If you don't want to bother with straining your lemonade, you can use this as a base for a smoothie or use frozen fruit to create a thicker lemonade treat.

Directions

JUICING METHOD

1. Rinse the berries and apples and prepare them according to your juicer's instructions.
2. Process all the ingredients.

BLENDER METHOD

1. Rinse the berries and apples.
2. Peel the apples. Core them and cut them into quarters.
3. Combine the berries, apples, and lemon in a high-speed blender and blend until smooth.
4. Put the blended fruit in a nut milk bag or fine strainer over a bowl.
5. Twist the top of the bag and squeeze to drain the juice into the bowl. If you're using a strainer, use a spoon to scrape the bottom to drain the juice.
6. Serve the juice over ice or chill in the refrigerator.

Strawberry Lemonade

There's nothing quite like fresh lemonade at the height of summer. If you love that tangy sweetness, adding fresh strawberries during strawberry season makes this epic. No fresh berries? No problem: You can use frozen, though I recommend using the blender method. No matter what you choose, you'll be sipping summer all year long.

DIFFICULTY
Easy

MAKES
2 servings

Ingredients

1 pint fresh strawberries

2 apples, cored and cut (see notes)

1 lemon, peeled

Notes

If you're using the blender method, peel your apples first.

If you don't want to bother with straining your lemonade, you can use this as a base for a smoothie or use frozen fruit to create a thicker lemonade treat.

Directions

JUICING METHOD

1. Rinse the berries and apples and prepare them according to your juicer's instructions.
2. Process all the ingredients.

BLENDER METHOD

1. Rinse the berries and apples.
2. Peel the apples. Core them and cut them into quarters.
3. Combine the berries, apples, and lemon in a high-speed blender and blend until smooth.
4. Put the blended fruit in a nut milk bag or fine strainer over a bowl.
5. Twist the top of the bag and squeeze to drain the juice into the bowl. If you're using a strainer, use a spoon to scrape the bottom to drain the juice.
6. Serve the juice over ice or chill in the refrigerator.

Pumpkin Spice Latte

This caffeine-free Pumpkin Spice Latte has all the coziness you'll need to get through the cooler seasons. Full of traditional autumn seasonings like ginger, clove, and cinnamon, it's also got the powerful anti-inflammatory turmeric to take it to another level. Craving this latte in the summer? You can enjoy it over ice too!

DIFFICULTY
Easy

MAKES
2 servings

Ingredients

1½ cups plant milk
⅓ cup pumpkin purée
3 Medjool dates, pitted
¼ teaspoon ground turmeric
¼ teaspoon ground cinnamon, plus a pinch as garnish
¼ teaspoon ground ginger
Pinch of ground cloves
Pinch of ground black pepper

Directions

1. Put all the ingredients in a high-speed blender and blend until smooth.
2. Put the blended ingredients in a small pot and warm over medium heat to desired temperature.
3. Pour into your favorite mug and sprinkle some extra cinnamon over the top.

Note

To enjoy this cold, pour over ice.

Creamy Chai

Chai is a traditional Indian milk beverage that dates back to ancient times. The spices can vary depending on who's preparing it, but almost always chai includes a good amount of green cardamom. Because spices contain so many beautiful health-promoting qualities, I love to create opportunities to include a variety of them whenever I can. This chai is one of those opportunities. To HV this one, I use a combination of plant milk and nut (or seed) butter for that extra creaminess.

DIFFICULTY
Easy

MAKES
2 servings

Ingredients

6 green cardamom pods

3–4 whole cloves

1–2 star anise

1 cup water

6 black peppercorns

3 slices fresh ginger root

½ stick cinnamon

1–2 tablespoons organic black tea (see notes)

1 cup plant milk

1 tablespoon nut or seed butter (see notes)

2–3 Medjool dates, pitted

Notes

For a caffeine-free version, use rooibos tea to replace the black tea.

Choose a nut or seed butter without any added oils or sweetener.

Directions

1. Using a mortar and pestle or mallet, lightly bruise the cardamom pods, cloves, and star anise by pounding them gently.
2. Bring the water to a light boil and add the peppercorns, ginger, and cinnamon stick.
3. Allow the chai base to simmer on low heat until reduced to half, about 15 minutes.
4. Add the black tea to your chai base, and simmer for 5 more minutes.
5. Remove from the heat and cover for 15 minutes.
6. Combine the chai base, plant milk, nut butter, and dates in a high-speed blender and blend until smooth.
7. For a cold version, serve over ice. For a hot mixture, return the chai to a pot and heat to your desired temperature.

Pumpkin Spice Latte
(page 129)

Creamy Chai
(page 130)

Golden Milk

This traditional Ayurvedic drink is a great beverage for treating yourself in the evenings as you're winding down from a long day. The main spice used here is turmeric, which not only gives this drink its name and golden color but also has all kinds of wonderful health-promoting qualities. I have also included an option to add nutmeg, since it has been shown to improve sleep duration and quality. So if you're in need of a good night's rest, or just a nice warm mug of health-promoting goodness, this one won't disappoint.

DIFFICULTY
Easy

MAKES
2 servings

Ingredients

1½ cups plant milk

½ teaspoon ground turmeric

⅛ teaspoon ground ginger

¼ teaspoon ground cinnamon, plus a pinch as garnish

Pinch of ground black pepper

1–2 Medjool dates, pitted

1 tablespoon nut or seed butter (see note)

⅛ teaspoon ground nutmeg (optional)

Note

Choose a nut butter without any added oils or sweetener.

Directions

1. Combine all the ingredients in a high-speed blender and blend until smooth.
2. Place the blended ingredients in a small pot and heat to your desired temperature.
3. Pour into your favorite mug and sprinkle some extra cinnamon on top.

Hot Chocolate

DIFFICULTY
Easy

MAKES
1 serving

What's more classic than a cup of hot chocolate? This healthy vegan version gets its sweetness from dates and its creaminess from the combination of plant milk and nut butter. This one definitely has all the rich and chocolatey goodness you'd expect!

Ingredients

1 cup water
1 tablespoon cashew butter (see note)
1 heaping tablespoon cocoa powder
2 Medjool dates, pitted

Directions

1. Combine all the ingredients in a high-speed blender and blend until smooth.
2. Transfer to a pot and heat to desired temperature.
3. Pour into your favorite mug.

Note

Choose cashew butter without any added oils or sweetener.

Matcha Latte

DIFFICULTY
Easy

MAKES
1 serving

The use of matcha dates back to ancient China but has become increasingly popular in the Western world in recent years. Matcha boasts some impressive health benefits, like improved cognitive function and cardio-metabolic health, and may inhibit the growth of tumors. Often picking up a matcha latte at a big-brand coffee shop means it contains high levels of refined sugar, artificial flavors, and additives. This healthy vegan version will enable you to make your own and know exactly what's in your cup!

Ingredients

1 cup plant milk
1–1½ teaspoons matcha powder
2 Medjool dates, pitted
¼ teaspoon vanilla extract
1 teaspoon nut or seed butter of choice (optional; see notes)

Directions

1. Combine all the ingredients in a high-speed blender and blend until smooth.
2. Transfer to a pot and heat over medium to desired temperature.

Notes

Choose a nut butter without any added oils or sweetener.

For a cold drink, enjoy it over ice.

SAND-WICHES AND WRAPS

There's nothing quite as satisfying as a delicious wrap or sandwich, and the recipes in this section make putting them together a breeze. Over the years, I've mastered the art of creating breads, plant-based veggie meats, and mouthwatering sauces, all with a healthy vegan twist. Now, I'm excited to share these techniques with you, showing you how to combine these wholesome components into flavorful and satisfying wraps and sandwiches. Whether you're hosting guests, feeding hungry teens, or simply treating yourself, these recipes are sure to be a hit!

No-Chick'n Caesar Wrap

Wraps are a great opportunity to add a variety of vegetables to one meal. The textures and flavors of this wrap are created using three of my favorite staples: my Chick'n-Style Mushrooms (page 34), my Creamy Caesar Dressing (page 62), and my Soft Almond Flatbread (page 51). As always, don't be afraid to load this one with greens, sprouts, and veggies of your choice to pump up the nutrition level!

DIFFICULTY
Easy

MAKES
2 wraps

Ingredients

2 cups Chick'n-Style Mushrooms (page 34)

2 Soft Almond Flatbreads (page 51)

TOPPINGS

Lettuce

Sprouts

Tomatoes

Avocado

½ cup Creamy Caesar Dressing (page 62)

Directions

1. Pile the Chick'n-Style Mushrooms onto your Soft Almond Flatbreads.
2. Top with lettuce, sprouts, tomatoes, and avocado. Top with Caesar dressing.

Island-Style Jerk Pulled Mushroom Wrap

I love to create healthier versions of classic foods, but I also love experimenting with combining different ingredients to create new flavors, and that's exactly what I did with this wrap. The combination of flavorful jerk sauce (page 61), plantain, and sweet fresh mango is amazing, but topping it off with Jalapeño Lime Sauce (page 60) adds a spicy zest that takes it to another level. If you're in the mood for something new, you've got to try this one!

DIFFICULTY
Easy

MAKES
2 wraps

Ingredients

12 ounces trumpet oyster or oyster mushrooms

½ cup Jerk Sauce (page 61)

½ ripe plantain (see note)

1 tablespoon coconut aminos

2 Soft Almond Flatbreads (page 51)

TOPPINGS

Fresh mango

Avocado

½ cup Jalapeño Lime Sauce (page 60)

Note

Plantain can be found at many conventional and ethnic grocery stores. Ripe plantains have black spots on them and are sweet in flavor. Although they resemble bananas, they have a much tougher skin, so you'll want to use a knife to make a lateral cut through the skin to remove it.

Directions

1. Preheat the oven to 425°F. Line a baking sheet with parchment paper.
2. Shred the mushrooms thinly and place in a skillet on medium-high. If they start to stick, add a splash of water until they release their own liquid. Continue to cook until the mushroom liquid has evaporated and the mushrooms begin to brown lightly in some areas, for 5 to 7 minutes.
3. Add the jerk sauce and mix. Remove from the heat.
4. Peel and cut the plantain into flat strips. Place the plantain on the parchment-lined baking sheet and brush with coconut aminos.
5. Bake at 425°F for 12 to 15 minutes
6. Assemble your wrap by adding the jerk mushrooms to your flatbread. Top with the baked plantain, fresh mango, and avocado. Drizzle with the Jalapeño Lime Sauce.

Pulled BBQ Jackfruit Sandwich

It often amazes me how whole food, plant-based ingredients can mimic the texture of meat. Young jackfruit is one of those ingredients; it works beautifully to create the texture of pulled pork. Here, I combine it with my Sweet Cherry BBQ Sauce (page 56) and a Gluten-Free Millet Burger Bun (page 52), topping it off with my Cabbage and Carrot Coleslaw. I have fed this to vegans and nonvegans, and both have been equally wowed!

DIFFICULTY
Easy

MAKES
4
sandwiches

Ingredients

4 Millet Burger Buns (page 52)

CABBAGE AND CARROT COLESLAW

½ cup MaYO (page 40)

1 tablespoon apple cider vinegar

1 tablespoon date paste (page 43)

¼ teaspoon garlic granules

½ cup finely sliced red cabbage

1 cup finely sliced green cabbage

¼ cup grated carrot

PULLED JACKFRUIT

2 (15-ounce) cans of young jackfruit (see note)

½–¾ cup Sweet Cherry BBQ Sauce (page 56)

¼ teaspoon ground black pepper

1 teaspoon garlic granules

½ teaspoon fennel powder

Salt and pepper to taste (optional)

Directions

1. Prepare the coleslaw by whisking together the mayo, apple cider vinegar, date paste, and garlic granules. Add the cabbage and carrot. Mix to combine.
2. Rough chop the jackfruit to the desired size.
3. Add the jackfruit to a pan and cook on medium heat for 1 to 2 minutes, or until the liquid evaporates.
4. Add the BBQ sauce, black pepper, garlic, and fennel. Mix and cook on medium heat for 5 to 7 minutes, or until the sauce is fragrant and thickens. Remove from the heat.
5. Add the jackfruit to your bun and top with the coleslaw. Season with salt and pepper, if using.

Note

If your jackfruit is canned in brine, you'll want to remove the flavor of brine before cooking. Empty both cans into a medium saucepan, boil for 10 minutes, and drain before using.

HV BLT

When I started healthy vegan eating, I knew I wanted to make favorite foods healthier for everyone. And bacon is one of those things, like cheese, that people don't want to give up! Well, this BLT checks all the flavor boxes without any of the downsides of pork. In this version, I'm layering my sweet and smoky Mushroom Bacon (page 85) on a Millet Burger Bun (page 52). I am keeping it classic with lettuce, tomato, and some of my MaYO (page 40), but you can amp up the nutritional level by using sprouts, microgreens, or any of your favorite veggies. The options are endless!

DIFFICULTY
Easy

MAKES
2 sandwiches

Ingredients

MaYO (page 40)

2 Millet Burger Buns (page 52), or 4 slices of High-Protein Loaf Bread (page 48)

Mushroom Bacon (page 85) (see note)

TOPPINGS

Lettuce

Tomatoes

Directions

1. Assemble your sandwich by spreading the MaYO on your bun. Add the mushroom bacon.
2. Top with lettuce, tomatoes, or other toppings.

Note

You will need only half a batch of Mushroom Bacon for this recipe. Store the other half in the fridge and use it to add a sweet and smoky crunch to any salad or sandwich.

Chickpea No-Tuna Salad Sandwich

This quick recipe comes together with ease and is a great high-protein meal. Ground nori sheets bring that seafood taste, combined with the other classic flavors of a tuna sandwich. This simple No-Tuna is perfect on top of a Millet Burger Bun (page 52) or my High-Protein Loaf Bread (page 48). Not in a sandwich mood? Pile it on top of a bowl of your favorite shredded greens.

DIFFICULTY
Easy

MAKES
4 servings

Ingredients

2⅔ cups cooked chickpeas, or 2 (15-ounce) cans chickpeas, drained and rinsed

1 tablespoon capers, chopped

½ cup MaYO (page 40)

1 tablespoon lemon juice

1 garlic clove, crushed

3 tablespoons ground nori (see notes)

1 teaspoon coconut aminos

⅓ cup diced celery

2 tablespoons diced red onion

½ teaspoon salt or to taste

Millet Burger Buns (page 52) or High-Protein Loaf Bread (page 48)

Directions

1. To prepare the no-tuna, put the chickpeas and capers in the food processor. Pulse a couple of times to break up the chickpeas. Take care not to overprocess or the mixture will get gummy.
2. Place the remaining ingredients in a bowl and mix.
3. Add the chickpea mixture to the bowl and mix to combine.
4. Top the bread with the no-tuna and other toppings of choice.

Notes

Store your no-tuna in the fridge for up to 5 days.

You can use oil-free packaged seaweed snacks in place of the nori.

No-Meatball Gyro

Traditionally a Greek dish, gyros have become quite popular throughout the world, so I wanted to include a healthy vegan alternative. If you're craving a meatless gyro, this is it. The veggie no-meatballs are made using my HV Veggie Ground (page 30), and of course we'll be adding my delicious cashew-based tzatziki sauce (page 63) and topping it with lettuce, tomatoes, and red onions to bring together the familiar Greek flavors, HV-style!

DIFFICULTY
Easy

MAKES
4 servings

Ingredients

VEGGIE NO-MEATBALLS

3 cups HV Veggie Ground (page 30)

4 tablespoons whole psyllium husks (see notes)

3 tablespoons arrowroot powder (see notes)

2 tablespoons chickpea flour (see notes)

½ teaspoon garlic granules

½ teaspoon salt or to taste

4 Soft Almond Flatbreads (page 51)

TOPPINGS

4 lettuce leaves

1 tomato, sliced

1 small red onion, sliced

1½ cups tzatziki sauce (page 63)

Directions

1. Preheat the oven to 350°F. Line a baking sheet with parchment paper and set aside.

2. Place the veggie no-meatball ingredients in a medium bowl and mix well.

3. Divide the mixture into 12 equal portions and roll into balls. Place the balls on the parchment-lined baking sheet. Bake for 20 minutes, or until crisp.

4. Assemble the gyros by placing 3 veggie no-meatballs on each flatbread. Top with lettuce, tomato, and onion and drizzle with tzatziki sauce.

Notes

The no-meatballs will keep in the fridge for 3 to 5 days; they can be frozen for 3 months.

Make sure to use whole psyllium husks for this recipe; using psyllium husk powder will result in a gummy texture.

Alternatively, you can bind these burgers using 3 to 4 tablespoons of chickpea flour and 1½ tablespoons of ground flaxseed instead of the arrowroot, but they will be a little less stable.

MYO Burrito

Depending on where you live, it can seem easier to just get takeout. But trust me, making your own is easy and, of course, healthier. For my version, I use pearl millet as a base, which is more nutrient dense than the commonly used white rice. Add in my HV Veggie Ground (page 30), seasonings, black beans, avocado, tomatoes, and, of course, my delicious cheese sauce (page 37), and you've got a classic burrito, MYO-style!

DIFFICULTY
Easy

MAKES
2 servings

Ingredients

1 cup cooked millet
½ cup cooked black beans
2 tablespoons tomato paste
¼ teaspoon garlic granules
½ teaspoon sweet paprika
¼ teaspoon onion granules
¼ teaspoon ground cumin
¼ teaspoon dried oregano
½ teaspoon salt or to taste

1 cup HV Veggie Ground (page 30)
2 Soft Almond Flatbreads (page 51; see note)

TOPPINGS

½ cup chopped tomato
½ avocado, sliced
½ cup Easy Cheese Sauce (page 37)

Directions

① In a medium bowl, place the millet, black beans, tomato paste, and spices and mix to combine.

② Build your burrito by spreading the millet mixture and veggie ground on a flatbread. Top with tomatoes and avocado. Drizzle with cheese sauce and roll up the bread.

③ You can warm this burrito in a pan or enjoy it at room temperature!

Note

When making your flatbread, you'll want to roll it a bit thinner than you would for a sandwich.

20-Minute Chickpea Tacos

Looking for a quick-and-easy, budget-friendly meal? These tacos are the perfect high-protein solution. They come together in under twenty minutes and are full of flavor! Here, I am using organic, sprouted corn tortillas, but these also pair well with my Soft Almond Flatbread (page 51).

DIFFICULTY
Easy

MAKES
4 servings

Ingredients

- 2⅔ cups cooked chickpeas, or 2 (15-ounce) cans chickpeas, drained and rinsed
- 1½ teaspoons dried oregano
- 1½ teaspoons smoked paprika
- 1½ teaspoons garlic granules
- ¾ teaspoon onion granules
- Cayenne pepper to taste
- 3 tablespoons coconut aminos
- ½ pint cherry tomatoes, or 1 small tomato, diced
- 6 sprouted organic corn tortillas (see notes)

TOPPINGS

- 2 avocados, mashed
- Fresh cilantro
- Classic Sour Cream (page 40)
- Squeeze of lime juice

Directions

1. Heat a skillet on medium and put in the chickpeas. Cook for 3 minutes or so, or until moisture from the chickpeas has mostly evaporated.
2. Add all the seasonings and coconut aminos. Continue to cook for 4 to 6 minutes until the excess liquid has evaporated and the chickpeas are nicely coated in the seasoning.
3. Add the cherry tomatoes and cook for another 3 to 5 minutes, or until the tomatoes are slightly shriveled. Remove from the heat.
4. Spread your tortillas with the chickpea filling and top with avocado or guacamole, cilantro, sour cream, and a squeeze of lime.

Notes

The chickpea filling will keep for up to 5 days in the fridge.

If you don't have tortillas or are avoiding corn, use my Soft Almond Flatbread (page 51).

The Better Bacon Cheeseburger

When transitioning to a plant-based diet, you may think you will never have a burger or bacon again—and you're right. But you can still create delicious and healthy vegan versions of your favorite foods, and this recipe is a testament to that! Using some of my favorite staples—Millet Burger Buns (page 52), HV Veggie Ground (page 30), Mushroom Bacon (page 85), and Easy Cheese Sauce (page 37)—you can create a delicious and satisfying whole food, plant-based burger.

DIFFICULTY
Easy

MAKES
2 servings

Ingredients

2 cups HV Veggie Ground (page 30)

2 tablespoons whole psyllium husks (see notes)

2 tablespoons arrowroot powder (see notes)

2 tablespoons chickpea flour (see notes)

2 teaspoons dried sage

½ teaspoon dried thyme

½ teaspoon garlic granules

Salt to taste

2 Millet Burger Buns (page 52)

TOPPINGS

6–8 pieces Mushroom Bacon (page 85)

½ cup Easy Cheese Sauce (page 37)

Directions

1. In a bowl, place the veggie ground, whole psyllium husks, arrowroot powder, chickpea flour, and seasonings and mix well. Form into patties.

2. Cook the patties on a well-seasoned cast-iron pan on medium heat for 5 to 7 minutes on each side, or until lightly browned. Alternatively, bake at 350°F for 20 to 30 minutes, flipping halfway through the baking. The patties should start to crisp on the outside.

3. Put the patties on the millet buns and top with Mushroom Bacon and cheese sauce.

Notes

These burgers can be cooked and stored for up to 5 days in the fridge or 2 months in the freezer.

Make sure to use whole psyllium husks for this recipe; using psyllium husk powder will result in a gummy texture.

Alternatively, you can bind these burgers using 2 to 3 tablespoons of chickpea flour and 1 tablespoon of ground flaxseed instead of the arrowroot, but they will be a little less stable.

Greek-Style Burger

Sometimes I'm in the mood for something unique yet familiar and that's exactly what you get with this Greek-Style Burger. I add kalamata olives, shallots, and fresh mint to my HV Veggie Ground (page 30) to create the burger and top it with my delicious tzatziki sauce (page 63). You know a burger is good when it's messy. This burger is messy!

DIFFICULTY
Easy

MAKES
2 servings

Ingredients

2 cups HV Veggie Ground (page 30)

2 tablespoons whole psyllium husks (see notes)

2 tablespoons arrowroot powder (see notes)

2 tablespoons chickpea flour (see notes)

1 garlic clove, minced

2 tablespoons minced shallots

1 teaspoon dried oregano

¼ cup halved kalamata olives

4 tablespoons chopped fresh mint

½ lime, juiced

Salt to taste

2 Millet Burger Buns (page 52)

TOPPINGS

Lettuce

Tomato

Red onion

1 cup tzatziki sauce (page 63)

Directions

1. In a bowl, place the veggie ground, whole psyllium husks, arrowroot powder, chickpea flour, and remaining ingredients and mix well. Form into patties.
2. Cook the patties in a well-seasoned cast-iron pan on medium heat for 5 to 7 minutes on each side, or until lightly browned. Alternatively, bake at 350°F for 20 to 30 minutes, flipping halfway through the baking. The patties should start to crisp on the outside.
3. Put the burgers on the buns and top with lettuce, tomato, red onion, and tzatziki sauce.

Notes

These burgers can be cooked and stored for up to 5 days in the fridge or 2 months in the freezer.

Make sure to use whole psyllium husks for this recipe; using psyllium husk powder will result in a gummy texture.

Alternatively, you can bind these burgers using 2 to 3 tablespoons of chickpea flour and 1 tablespoon of ground flaxseed instead of the arrowroot, but they will be a little less stable.

SALADS, BOWLS, AND SOUPS

When many people think of healthy vegan eating, they think of endless bowls of boring greens or food that tastes like indescribable "health food." I am here to change that! As much as I love burgers, there is definitely a place for salads, bowls, and soups. I have a salad every day, and when people ask me for a good starting place for improving their diet, I suggest they do the same! These recipes are a great place to start.

Curry Chickpea Tahini Bowl

Salads and bowls are a great way to include a variety of nutrient-dense foods in one dish, and this bowl does just that. Quinoa, veggies, and flavor-packed curry chickpeas are all topped off with a delicious sweet and tangy tahini dressing. This bowl makes a perfectly healthy lunch or dinner!

DIFFICULTY
Easy

MAKES
2 servings

Ingredients

1⅓ cups cooked chickpeas, or 1 (15-ounce) can chickpeas

1 teaspoon curry powder

2 tablespoons coconut aminos

Salt and pepper to taste (optional)

1 cup broccoli florets

2 cups cooked quinoa or millet

TAHINI DRESSING

¼ cup tahini

¼–½ cup water

1 garlic clove

2 tablespoons lemon juice

3 Medjool dates, pitted

¼ teaspoon salt or to taste

TOPPINGS

½ cup sliced bell pepper

½ cup grated carrot

Directions

1. Preheat the oven to 375°F. Line a baking sheet with parchment paper.

2. Drain the chickpeas but do not rinse them. Put them in a medium bowl with the curry powder, coconut aminos, and salt and pepper, if using. Toss to mix.

3. Spread the chickpeas out on the parchment-lined baking sheet. Bake for 10 to 15 minutes, or until the chickpeas have reached your desired texture.

4. Steam the broccoli in a steamer, or add a ¼ cup of water to the bottom of a saucepan along with the broccoli florets. Cover and simmer on medium-low for 5 to 10 minutes, or until the broccoli is cooked to your preferred texture. Remember, less cooking equals more nutrients!

5. Combine all the dressing ingredients in a high-speed blender and blend until smooth.

6. Put the quinoa in a bowl and top with the roasted curry chickpeas, bell pepper, and carrot. Drizzle generously with the tahini dressing.

Note

Store the chickpeas and quinoa in the fridge for 3 days. The dressing will also keep for up to 5 days in the fridge.

Portobello Steak and Ranch Salad

Portobello mushrooms are great to use when you are looking for a denser meaty texture. They can be found at most grocery stores and are quick and easy to season and add to salads like this one. The spices here are simple: onion and garlic granules, smoked paprika, and some coconut aminos. Don't forget to top this with my Creamy Dill Ranch Dressing (page 65) for my take on a classic steak salad.

DIFFICULTY
Easy

MAKES
2 servings

Portobello Steaks

- 1 tablespoon coconut aminos
- 1 teaspoon dried sage
- ½ teaspoon garlic granules
- ½ teaspoon onion granules
- ¼ teaspoon ground black pepper
- ½ teaspoon smoked paprika
- 2 large portobello mushroom caps

Veggies

- 2 cups mixed greens
- ½ pint cherry tomatoes, halved, or 1 medium tomato, chopped
- ⅓ cup sliced bell peppers
- ¼ cup sliced red onions
- ¼ cup kalamata olives or olives of your choice
- ½ cup Creamy Dill Ranch Dressing (page 65)

Note

The mushrooms will keep for 3 days in the fridge.

Directions

(1) Whisk the coconut aminos and spices together and set aside.

(2) Heat a well-seasoned cast-iron pan on medium-low. Place 2 large portobello caps on the pan and then place a heavy-bottom pan or burger press on top of the mushrooms.

(3) As the mushrooms begin to cook, gently create pressure by pressing down on the pan or burger press. This will encourage water to release from the portobellos and create a denser texture.

(4) Cook the mushrooms for 3 to 5 minutes to release water, then increase the temperature to medium-high.

(5) Continue to cook the first side of the mushrooms for about 5 minutes, or until most of the excess water has evaporated.

(6) Flip the mushrooms and continue to cook them, using the pressing technique, for another 5 minutes, or until the remaining water evaporates.

(7) Once the portobello caps are cooked, pour on the seasoning mixture, coating the front and back of the caps; then cook them for 2 to 3 minutes, or until no more liquid remains. Remove from the heat.

(8) Slice the portobello mushrooms into strips.

(9) In a large bowl, combine all the vegetables for the salad. Top with the portobello mushrooms and add the ranch dressing.

Nacho Salad Bowl

Eating healthy does not mean forgoing nachos! This one is for all the nacho lovers out there: a combination of crispy oven-baked tortilla chips, fresh veggies, sweet potatoes, black beans, avocado, and HV Veggie Ground (page 30), all topped off with a delicious Jalapeño Cheese Sauce. Now you can satisfy that nacho craving and nourish your body at the same time.

DIFFICULTY
Easy

MAKES
4 servings

Ingredients

4 organic sprouted corn tortillas

5 lettuce leaves of choice, chopped

1 small sweet potato, diced and steamed

½ cup cooked black beans

⅓ cup diced red pepper

¼ cup diced red onion

1 cup halved cherry tomatoes, or 1 medium tomato, chopped

½ cup chopped cilantro

½ avocado, sliced

2 cups HV Veggie Ground (page 30)

Squeeze of lime juice

JALAPEÑO CHEESE SAUCE

2 roasted jalapeños

¾ cup raw cashews

1 Medjool date, pitted

3 tablespoons nutritional yeast

¼ teaspoon sweet paprika

⅛ teaspoon ground turmeric

⅛ teaspoon ground cumin

¼ teaspoon garlic granules

¼ teaspoon salt or to taste

½ cup water

Directions

① Preheat the oven to 350°F.

② Cut the tortillas into desired chip shapes. Spread them out on a baking sheet, taking care not to overlap them. Bake for 10 to 12 minutes, or until crisp. Remove from the heat and cool. Adjust the oven temperature to 400°F.

③ Bake the whole jalapeños for 20 minutes, or until some dark spots appear and the jalapeños are soft.

④ Combine the cheese sauce ingredients in a high-speed blender and blend until smooth. Set aside.

⑤ Place the lettuce on a large plate or platter. Top with the tortilla chips. Continue to layer the sweet potato, black beans, and the rest of the veggies, along with the veggie ground. Finally, top with the cheese sauce and a squeeze of lime.

Notes

Cheese sauce will keep for up to 5 days in the fridge.

For a nut-free Jalapeño Cheese Sauce, sub cashews with half cannellini beans and half raw sunflower seeds.

Sushi Salad Bowl, aka the World's Easiest Sushi

If you love sushi and find the idea of rolling your own intimidating or too time-consuming, this bowl is the perfect solution. Instead of rice, it calls for sushi-style quinoa and an assortment of veggies (and fruit) and is topped off with Spicy Mayo, crushed nori sheets, and toasted sesame seeds. With this distinct Japanese flavor profile, you won't miss the fish!

DIFFICULTY
Easy

MAKES
4 bowls

Ingredients

BOWL

4 tablespoons coconut aminos

3 tablespoons apple cider vinegar

1 tablespoon date syrup (see notes)

1 teaspoon grated fresh ginger

4 cups cooked quinoa

½ cup shredded purple cabbage

½ cup grated carrot

½ cup diced red pepper

½ cup diced cucumber

1 avocado, diced

1 cup diced mango

¼ cup toasted sesame seeds

4 nori sheets, cut into quarters or crushed

SPICY MAYO

½ cup MaYO (page 40)

1 tablespoon date-sweetened sriracha (see notes)

½ tablespoon coconut aminos

Directions

1. In a large bowl, place the coconut aminos, apple cider vinegar, date syrup, and ginger. Add the quinoa to the bowl and mix to combine.

2. Add all the diced vegetables and mango to the quinoa and mix to combine.

3. Combine the Spicy Mayo ingredients.

4. Serve topped with the spicy mayo, sesame seeds, and nori. You can also use a nori sheet to roll this salad into a sushi burrito!

Notes

The quinoa mixture will keep in the fridge for 3 days. The spicy mayo will keep in the fridge for up to 5 days.

You may substitute the date syrup with 1½ tablespoons of date paste (page 43).

You can find date-sweetened sriracha at health-food stores and online.

Super Seven Power Salad

An ode to Dr. Fuhrman's GBOMBS, this salad contains a combination of food categories that have been shown to not only be health promoting but also prevent disease: leafy greens, beans, onions, mushrooms, nuts and/or seeds, and berries. Dr. Fuhrman recommends consuming GBOMBS every day. My favorite way to top this salad is with my Sweet Dijon Dressing (page 66), but you can use any of the delicious dressings featured in this book for a nutritionally powerful meal.

DIFFICULTY
Easy

MAKES
2–3 servings

Ingredients

2 cups chopped lettuce(s) of choice

1 cup finely chopped kale

1 cup cooked chickpeas

1 cup halved cherry tomatoes

1 cup grated carrots

½ cup diced onions

1 cup cooked mushrooms of choice (see note)

2 tablespoons hemp hearts

½ cup pomegranate seeds

1 cup fresh blueberries

Dressing of choice

Directions

① Place all the salad ingredients in a large bowl and gently mix to combine.

② Sprinkle the hemp hearts, pomegranate seeds, and blueberries over the top. Drizzle with your dressing of choice.

Note

Try the mushrooms from the Portobello Steak and Ranch Salad (page 163) here.

Sweet Dijon Pasta Salad

Looking for a simple dish to bring to your next dinner party or cookout? You know the kind of dish you can enjoy and be satisfied with even if none of the other food meets your dietary style? This is it. While you can use conventional pasta, lentil or chickpea pasta provides a nice, unrefined boost of protein. The combination of vegetables with my walnut-based Sweet Dijon Dressing (page 66) will have you and your friends going back for seconds.

DIFFICULTY
Easy

MAKES
2–3 servings

Ingredients

8 ounces lentil or chickpea pasta (about 270 grams)

3 cups chopped arugula

¼ cup chopped fresh parsley

½ pint cherry tomatoes, halved

¼ cup diced red onion

⅓ cup halved kalamata olives, pitted

1 recipe of Sweet Dijon Dressing (page 66)

Directions

1. Cook the pasta according to package directions until al dente. Drain.
2. In a large bowl, combine the pasta with the arugula, parsley, tomatoes, onion, and olives. Add the dressing and mix. Enjoy!

Note

This will keep in the fridge for 3 days.

Sweet Potato Curry Soup

The combination of curry with the extra kick of fresh ginger makes this the perfect soup to have on a cool fall day. Pair it with a slice of High-Protein Loaf Bread (page 48) or any of the sandwiches in this book for a complete and satisfying meal—the ultimate comfort food!

DIFFICULTY
Easy

MAKES
4 servings

Ingredients

- 4 medium sweet potatoes
- 2 small yellow onions, peeled and halved
- 3 cups salt-free vegetable broth or water
- 2 teaspoons curry powder
- 1-inch piece fresh turmeric root, peeled (see notes)
- ½-inch piece fresh ginger root, peeled (see notes)
- 2 garlic cloves, roughly chopped
- 1½ teaspoons salt or to taste
- Roasted chickpeas, for garnish (optional; see notes)
- Microgreens, for garnish (optional)

Directions

1. Preheat the oven to 400°F.
2. Poke holes in the sweet potatoes with a fork. Place the potatoes and onion halves on a baking sheet and bake for 30 to 45 minutes, or until the potatoes can be easily pierced with a fork and the onion is soft and slightly browned.
3. Combine the sweet potatoes, onions, and the remaining ingredients in a high-speed blender and blend until smooth.
4. Transfer the blended soup to a pot and heat until hot.
5. Garnish with roasted chickpeas and microgreens, if using.

Notes

This soup will keep for 5 days in the fridge and 3 months in the freezer.

If you can't find fresh turmeric and ginger root, you can use ½ teaspoon of ground turmeric and ¼ teaspoon of ground ginger.

For quick roasted chickpeas, take one 15-ounce can of chickpeas, drain, rinse, and pat dry. Add 1 tablespoon of coconut aminos and toss. Roast on a baking sheet at 375°F for 15 to 20 minutes, or until crisp. For an even quicker method, you can cook the chickpeas in a skillet. They won't be as crisp, but they will still be a tasty garnish.

Chunky Vegetable Tomato Soup

Nothing says autumn quite like a good hearty tomato vegetable soup. This version has a thick, saucy base; I like cutting the vegetables into larger chunks to add extra texture. This soup is satisfying enough for a meal, but you can also enjoy a bowl as a side dish with my Chickpea No-Tuna Salad Sandwich (page 146) or HV BLT (page 145).

DIFFICULTY
Easy

MAKES
4 servings

Ingredients

- 1 small yellow onion, diced
- 4 garlic cloves, minced
- 3 cups diced celery
- 2 small red potatoes, diced
- 1½ cups diced carrots
- 1 cup chopped green beans, cut into 1-inch pieces
- 15 ounces diced or puréed tomatoes
- 1 (6- to 7-ounce) jar tomato paste (see notes)
- 3 tablespoons date paste (page 43)
- 1 tablespoon Italian seasoning
- 1 tablespoon dried basil
- 1 teaspoon dried oregano
- 1 bay leaf
- 1 quart low-sodium or salt-free vegetable broth
- ½ bunch kale, chopped
- ½ cup cashew or coconut cream (optional; see notes)
- 1 tablespoon dried parsley
- 2 teaspoons salt or to taste
- ½ teaspoon ground black pepper
- ½ lemon, juiced (optional)

Directions

① Begin by pouring a small amount of water or vegetable broth in a soup pot. On medium heat, sauté the onions, garlic, and celery for 5 to 7 minutes, or until the veggies are soft. Add a little more water or broth as necessary to prevent sticking.

② Add the potatoes, carrots, and green beans. Sauté for 3 to 5 minutes, or until the veggies start to soften. Add the diced tomatoes, tomato paste, date paste, and all seasonings except for the parsley, salt, and black pepper. Stir to combine. Keep stirring to prevent sticking. Continue to stir while the tomatoes and veggies cook for 3 minutes.

③ Add the vegetable broth. Cover and simmer for 15 to 20 minutes, or until the veggies are tender and a fork pierces a potato easily. Add the kale and stir.

④ Stir in the cashew cream. Add the parsley, salt, black pepper, and lemon juice, if using. Mix and simmer for a few additional minutes. Enjoy!

Notes

Store this soup in the fridge for up to 5 days or in the freezer for 3 months.

Since tomatoes are acidic and can have a reaction with the metal in cans, I prefer to purchase my tomato paste in a glass jar.

Cashew cream can be made by blending ¼ cup of soaked raw cashews with ½ cup of water until smooth.

NUT-FREE: Substitute full-fat coconut milk for cashew cream.

HV Cheddar Broccoli Soup

This Cheddar Broccoli Soup packs all the flavor of a traditional version but, of course, HV-style: Instead of dairy, I use a base of butternut squash, raw cashews, and hemp hearts to create the rich creaminess and nutritional yeast and apple cider vinegar to give it the perfect cheesy flavor. Pair this soup with a slice of my High-Protein Loaf Bread (page 48) or any of the delicious sandwiches or wraps in this book.

DIFFICULTY
Easy

MAKES
4 servings

Ingredients

6 cups chopped broccoli florets cut into small, bite-size pieces and stalks cut into 1-inch pieces, divided

1 small onion, diced

4–5 garlic cloves, minced

5 cups seeded, peeled, and cubed butternut squash (about 1½ pounds)

1 tablespoon Dijon mustard

1 teaspoon apple cider vinegar

2½ teaspoons salt

4 cups salt-free vegetable broth or water

⅓ cup raw cashews (see notes)

⅓ cup hemp hearts

6 tablespoons nutritional yeast (see notes)

1 teaspoon ground turmeric

½ teaspoon ground black pepper

Notes

Store this soup in the fridge for 3 days or in the freezer for 1 month.

If you're avoiding nutritional yeast, use 2 to 3 tablespoons of miso paste and reduce the salt to your taste.

NUT-FREE: Replace cashews with raw sunflower seeds.

Directions

① Lightly steam 2 cups of broccoli by placing them in a pot with ½ cup of water. Cover and simmer for 5 minutes, or just until the broccoli can be pierced with a fork. The broccoli should brighten in color when it's ready. Drain any water that remains at the bottom of the pot and set aside.

② In a stockpot, place the onion and garlic and ¼ cup of water. Sauté for 5 minutes, or until soft. Add the squash, remaining broccoli (4 cups), Dijon mustard, apple cider vinegar, and salt. Sauté for 3 to 5 minutes.

③ Add the broth and simmer, covered, for about 7 minutes, or until the squash is soft. Turn off the heat.

④ Add the cashews and hemp hearts and let sit until the soup is cool enough to blend.

⑤ Place the soup in a high-speed blender along with the nutritional yeast, turmeric, and black pepper, and blend until smooth.

⑥ Transfer back to the pot and heat. Add the steamed broccoli and mix. Enjoy with a slice of bread.

MAIN DISHES

I once thought I could never give up meat. I loved chicken. I loved beef. I simply couldn't fathom giving up the flavors of dishes made with meat to become vegan. Well, now I am telling you . . . you don't have to! This is because the flavors that you are accustomed to when eating meat dishes are primarily created by the seasonings that are put on them. I have shocked and amazed people by giving them what looks and tastes like a chicken sandwich, lasagna, sausage patty, or meatloaf, only to reveal that what they were actually eating, and loving, was my vegan version of those dishes. I have created recipes that use mushrooms and other super-healthy foods to create the same meaty texture that people who eat meat are accustomed to. And by adding the proper seasonings, you can create the perfect flavors to complement the texture, creating a healthy vegan version of all your favorite meat dishes. I know you will love these main dishes, and I am excited to share these recipes with you!

Sticky Teriyaki Cauliflower Wings

Cauliflower is having its day and with good reason. Not only is it packed full of nutrients, but it also takes to sauces like a champ and makes a perfect wing. Serve these flavorful wings as finger food for your next gathering or turn them into a satisfying meal by pairing them with wholesome grains like millet, quinoa, or your favorite noodles. If teriyaki isn't your thing, try my Sweet Cherry BBQ Sauce (page 56) instead.

DIFFICULTY
Easy

MAKES
4 servings

Ingredients

2 cups unsweetened plant milk

4 teaspoons ground flaxseed

½ cup oat flour

Wheat-Free Breadcrumbs (page 46) or Extra Crunchy Wheat-Free Breadcrumbs (page 47)

2 medium heads cauliflower, cut into florets

Teriyaki Sauce (page 60)

Black and white sesame seeds, for garnish

Notes

These are best eaten right away.

The wet mixture will thicken as it sits; thin it by adding small amounts of plant milk and mixing.

These wings are also delicious with Sweet Cherry BBQ Sauce (page 56), Spicy Mango Buffalo Sauce (page 57), and Jerk Sauce (page 61).

Directions

1. Preheat the oven to 375°F. Line a baking sheet with parchment paper.
2. In a bowl, place the plant milk, ground flaxseed, and oat flour and whisk to combine. Set aside for 5 minutes. Pour the breadcrumbs onto a plate.
3. Prepare a dipping station: Place the bowl of wet ingredients next to the plate of breadcrumbs. Lastly, place the parchment-lined baking sheet next to the breadcrumbs.
4. Dip the cauliflower florets in the wet mixture and then coat them with the breadcrumbs. Place them onto the baking sheet. Make sure the florets don't overlap.
5. Bake for 20 minutes, or until golden. Remove the cauliflower wings from the oven and brush generously with the teriyaki sauce.
6. Return the wings to the oven and continue to bake for an additional 15 minutes, or until they look sticky.
7. Brush with extra teriyaki sauce and sprinkle with sesame seeds.

Mango Buffalo Mushroom Wings

Mushrooms are truly having a renaissance, and with good reason: They are high in nutrients and are rapidly becoming one of the more popular meat alternatives. They are simple to cook with and absorb flavor easily, and they also have an undeniably meaty texture. Although these wings are best when made with oyster or maitake mushrooms, if you're in an area where they are difficult to find, you can also make this recipe using lion's mane mushrooms. Whatever you choose, don't forget to make a batch of my Creamy Dill Ranch Dressing (page 65) for dipping!

DIFFICULTY
Easy

MAKES
4 servings

Ingredients

2 cups unsweetened plant milk

4 teaspoons ground flaxseed

½ cup oat flour

Wheat-Free Breadcrumbs (page 46) or Extra Crunchy Wheat-Free Breadcrumbs (page 47)

1½ pounds oyster, maitake, or lion's mane mushrooms, broken into pieces (see notes)

Spicy Mango Buffalo Sauce (page 57; see notes)

Notes

These are best eaten right away.

Lion's mane mushrooms contain more water than oyster mushrooms. If you're using lion's mane mushrooms, you will need to break them into smaller 2-inch pieces and bake them for an additional 15 minutes.

Wet mixture will thicken as it sits; thin it by adding small amounts of plant milk as necessary.

These wings are also delicious with Sweet Cherry BBQ Sauce (page 56), Jerk Sauce (page 61), and Teriyaki Sauce (page 60).

Directions

1. Preheat the oven to 375°F. Line a baking sheet with parchment paper.
2. In a bowl, place the plant milk, ground flaxseed, and oat flour and whisk to combine. Set aside for 5 minutes. Pour the breadcrumbs onto a plate.
3. Prepare a dipping station: Place the bowl of wet ingredients next to the plate of breadcrumbs. Lastly, place your parchment-lined baking sheet next to the breadcrumbs
4. Dip the mushroom clusters in the wet mixture and then coat them with the breadcrumbs. Place them on the baking sheet. Make sure the clusters don't overlap.
5. Bake for 10 to 15 minutes, or until dark golden. Remove the mushroom wings and flip each one over.
6. Return the wings to the oven and continue to bake for an additional 10 to 15 minutes.
7. Remove the wings from the oven and brush generously with the buffalo sauce. Return them to the oven and bake for an additional 10 minutes.
8. Remove from the oven, if needed, brush with extra buffalo sauce, and serve.

Portobello Fajitas

The first time I made these fajitas, I was amazed at how simple and flavorful they turned out. Slicing the portobello mushrooms into strips creates the perfect texture and mouthfeel, and the smoked paprika and coconut aminos have a slightly sweet and smoky flavor. Serve these on my Soft Almond Flatbread (page 51) and top them with Easy Cheese Sauce (page 37) or some Jalapeño Lime Sauce (page 60)!

DIFFICULTY
Easy

MAKES
4 servings

Ingredients

- 12 ounces portobello mushrooms
- 3 tablespoons coconut aminos
- 1 tablespoon sweet paprika
- 1 teaspoon smoked paprika
- 2 teaspoons ground cumin
- 2 teaspoons garlic granules
- 1 teaspoon onion granules
- ½ red onion, cut into strips
- 1 bell pepper, cut into strips
- ½–1 jalapeño, seeded and minced
- 1 teaspoon salt or to taste (optional)
- 4 Soft Almond Flatbreads (page 51)
- 1 avocado, sliced
- ⅓ cup Easy Cheese Sauce (page 37)

Directions

1. Slice the mushrooms into strips and place in a bowl. Add the coconut aminos and seasonings. Mix and set aside.
2. In a skillet, heat ¼ cup of water on medium-high. Add the red onion strips and cook them for about 5 minutes, or until they begin to soften.
3. Add the mushrooms and allow to cook for 3 to 5 minutes, or until the liquid from the mushrooms has released and mostly cooked off.
4. Add the bell pepper and jalapeño to the skillet. Continue to cook for another 3 to 5 minutes, or until the peppers are cooked but not too soft. Add salt, if using. Remove from the heat.
5. Place the portobello mixture on the flatbreads. Top with sliced avocado and cheese sauce. Enjoy!

Note

Portobello mixture will keep for 3 days in the fridge.

Sweet Potato Chili Cheese Fries

This recipe is another great example of how classic dishes can be re-created using healthier whole food ingredients. My twist transforms traditional chili cheese fries into a wholesome dish by using baked sweet potato fries, Three-Bean Chili (page 189), and HV Veggie Ground (page 30) and topping it all off with some Easy Cheese Sauce (page 37). I told you eating healthy doesn't mean giving up your favorites—now you know!

DIFFICULTY
Easy

MAKES
2 generous servings

Ingredients

3 medium sweet potatoes, peeled and sliced

½ teaspoon salt (optional)

2 cups Three-Bean Chili (page 189)

1 cup HV Veggie Ground (page 30)

1 cup Easy Cheese Sauce (page 37)

Directions

1. You can either bake or air-fry the fries. If baking, preheat the oven to 400°F. Line a baking sheet with parchment paper and set aside.
2. Cut the sweet potatoes into french fries. Add salt, if using, and mix to coat.
3. Place the fries on the parchment-lined baking sheet and bake for 30 minutes, flipping halfway. If air-frying, transfer fries to an air-frying basket and air-fry at 350°F for 10 to 15 minutes.
4. Combine the Three-Bean Chili with the HV Veggie Ground and mix.
5. Place the cooked fries in a serving dish and top them with chili and cheese sauce.
6. Optionally, bake for an additional 15 minutes. Enjoy!

Three-Bean Chili

Beans have gotten a bad rap in some circles, but I am here to tell you that they are heart-healthy and full of fiber and protein and really make dishes like this stand out. My secret ingredients here are jalapeño and date paste—the heat and sweet offset each other, blending with the rest of the spices for a chili that can hold its own with the best of them. This chili is a hearty flavorful bowl of goodness on its own, but you can also take it up a notch by adding some HV Veggie Ground (page 30) or by topping it off with some Classic Sour Cream (page 40).

DIFFICULTY
Easy

MAKES
4 servings

Ingredients

1⁄3 cup water (for cooking)

1 medium red onion, diced

2 garlic cloves, minced

1 red pepper, diced

2 carrots, diced

2 celery stalks, diced

1 jalapeño, minced

1 bay leaf

1½ tablespoons sweet paprika

1 teaspoon smoked paprika

3 teaspoons ground cumin

2 teaspoons dried oregano

1 teaspoon garlic granules

2½ cups diced tomatoes

3 cups cooked beans (I used black, pinto, and kidney, but you can use whatever you prefer)

1 teaspoon salt or to taste

2 tablespoons date paste (page 43)

2 tablespoons fresh cilantro

½ lime, juiced

1 avocado, sliced

Easy Cheese Sauce (page 37)

Classic Sour Cream (page 40)

Directions

1. Place the water in a large stockpot and heat on medium-high. Add the onion and garlic. Let cook for 3 minutes, or until the onions are soft.

2. Add the veggies (except the tomatoes), bay leaf, paprika, cumin, oregano, and garlic granules. Mix and allow to cook on medium-low heat for 5 minutes, or until the veggies are tender but still firm.

3. Add the tomatoes, beans, salt, and date paste. Cover and let simmer on low for 30 minutes.

4. Add the cilantro and lime and mix. Serve with avocado, a drizzle of cheese sauce, and a dollop of sour cream.

Note

If you like your chili extra saucy, blend ¾ cup of the chili until smooth and add it back to the pan before adding the cilantro and lime.

No-Crab Cakes

Not only do hearts of palm help give these cakes the perfect crab-cake texture, but they are also rich in minerals potassium, iron, copper, phosphorus, and zinc. Hearts of palm also contain a fair amount of plant protein. To bring the flavor of the sea, I use ground nori or dulse flakes and all the seasonings you'd expect from a great No-Crab Cake. For you sauce lovers, I've included my tartar sauce and cocktail sauce recipes. . . . The choice is yours.

DIFFICULTY
Easy

MAKES
6 servings

Ingredients

CAKES

1⅓ cups cooked chickpeas, or 1 (15-ounce) can chickpeas, drained and rinsed

2 (15-ounce) cans hearts of palm

½ cup MaYO (page 40)

1 tablespoon coconut aminos

2 teaspoons lemon juice

1 teaspoon Dijon mustard

2 teaspoons ground nori or dulse flakes

1 tablespoon dried parsley

2 teaspoons seafood seasoning (like Old Bay)

1 teaspoon garlic granules

½ teaspoon salt or to taste

½ cup chopped green onions

2 cups Wheat-Free Breadcrumbs (page 46) or Extra Crunchy Wheat-Free Breadcrumbs, divided (page 47)

TARTAR SAUCE

½ cup MaYO (page 40)

1 tablespoon lemon juice

1 tablespoon chopped fresh dill (see notes)

1 teaspoon coconut aminos

1 teaspoon Dijon mustard

1 small pickle, chopped

2 tablespoons capers, chopped

Salt and pepper to taste

COCKTAIL SAUCE

½ cup tomato paste

2 tablespoons date paste (page 43)

1 teaspoon apple cider vinegar

1 tablespoon lemon juice

1 teaspoon coconut aminos

2 tablespoons horseradish

1 teaspoon hot sauce or to taste

¼ teaspoon salt or to taste

Directions

① Put the chickpeas and hearts of palm in a food processor. Pulse until the hearts of palm are shredded with some bigger pieces throughout.

② In a large bowl, place the MaYO, coconut aminos, lemon juice, Dijon mustard, ground nori, dried parsley, seafood seasoning, garlic granules, and salt and mix to combine.

③ Add the chickpea mixture, green onions, and half the breadcrumbs and mix to combine.

④ Form the mixture into 6 cakes and coat each side of the cakes with the remaining breadcrumbs.

(recipe continues)

No-Crab Cakes (continued)

⑤ Prepare the tartar and/or cocktail sauce. Combine each set of ingredients separately in two bowls.

⑥ Heat a well-seasoned cast-iron skillet on medium-low. Cook the cakes for 5 to 7 minutes on each side, or until lightly golden. I have found that cooking at a lower temperature helps prevent sticking when avoiding oil. Serve with tartar and/or cocktail sauce.

Notes

The tartar sauce will keep in the fridge for 3 to 5 days. The cocktail sauce will keep in the fridge for 5 days.

For the tartar sauce, you can use dried dill in a pinch.

Grilled Portobello Pasta with Cilantro Pea Pesto

This recipe is full of plant-based protein, thanks to the combination of chickpea pasta, peas, and pumpkin seeds. To make it even better, it's topped with marinated, pan-grilled portobello mushrooms, making it both hearty and satisfying, once again proving that comfort food can also be nourishing.

DIFFICULTY
Easy

MAKES
2 generous servings

Ingredients

4 portobello caps

2 cups Cilantro Pea Pesto (page 67)

8 ounces lentil or chickpea pasta (about 270 grams)

MARINADE

½ cup oil-free, salt-free vegetable broth

¼ cup coconut aminos

1 teaspoon garlic granules

½ teaspoon onion granules

½ teaspoon smoked paprika

Directions

1. Heat a well-seasoned cast-iron pan on medium-low. Place 2 large portobello caps on the pan. Place a heavy-bottom pan or burger press on top of the mushrooms.

2. As the mushrooms begin to cook, gently create pressure by pressing down on the pan or burger press. This will encourage water to release from the portobellos and create a denser texture.

3. Cook the mushrooms for 3 to 5 minutes to release water; then increase the temperature to medium-high. Continue to cook the first side of the mushrooms for about 5 minutes, or until most of the excess water has evaporated.

4. Flip the mushrooms and continue to cook them, using the pressing technique, for another 5 minutes, or until the remaining water evaporates. Remove them from the pan.

5. Prepare the marinade by combining all the ingredients in a flat-bottom deep dish. Add the cooked portobello mushrooms and allow them to marinate for 20 minutes while preparing the pesto and cooking the pasta.

6. Prepare the pesto. Boil the pasta according to package instructions. Drain and set aside.

(recipe continues)

Grilled Portobello Pasta with Cilantro Pea Pesto (continued)

⑦ Heat the cast-iron pan on medium. Place the marinated portobellos in the pan and cook for 3 to 5 minutes, or until they have released their water and the water has cooked off. Flip the mushrooms as necessary. For added flavor, pour a couple of tablespoons of the marinade over the mushrooms as they're cooking in the pan. The mushrooms are ready once the excess moisture has evaporated.

⑧ Mix the pesto with the cooked pasta. Slice the portobello mushrooms and add them to your dish.

Mushroom Medley Pasta

This rich and creamy dish is an elevated take on a vegan Alfredo. Topped with a delicious medley of seasoned portobellos, shiitakes, and white mushrooms, you won't believe that something this simple to make can taste so good! Serve this alongside a Super Seven Power Salad (page 168) and maybe even a slice of High-Protein Loaf Bread (page 48).

DIFFICULTY
Easy

MAKES
3 generous portions

Ingredients

8 ounces lentil or chickpea pasta (about 270 grams)

MUSHROOMS

- 4 ounces sliced portobello mushrooms
- 4 ounces sliced white mushrooms
- 4 ounces sliced shiitake mushrooms
- 2 teaspoons garlic granules
- 1 teaspoon onion granules
- 1 teaspoon dried parsley
- 1 teaspoon sweet paprika
- Salt and pepper to taste

SAUCE

- 1¼ cups raw cashews, soaked for at least 2 hours
- 2 cups water or more as needed
- 2 garlic cloves
- 2 teaspoons salt or to taste
- Ground black pepper to taste

Fresh Italian flat-leaf parsley, for garnish

Wheat-Free Breadcrumbs (page 46), for garnish (optional)

Directions

1. Boil the pasta according to the package directions. Drain and set aside.
2. In a medium-size skillet, pour a little water and sauté the mushrooms on high until almost all the water is cooked off. Add the seasonings and cook for an additional 2 to 3 minutes. Add more water if necessary to prevent sticking. Remove from the heat.
3. Drain the cashews and discard the soaking water. Combine the cashews and other sauce ingredients in a high-speed blender and blend until smooth. Adjust the thickness of the sauce by adding small amounts of water as necessary.
4. Pour the sauce in a stockpot and heat just until it bubbles, for about 2 minutes. The sauce will thicken when heated. Add the prepared noodles and mix until they are coated.
5. Add the pasta to a plate and top with the mushrooms, parsley, and breadcrumbs, if using. Enjoy!

Note

NUT-FREE: Use one 15-ounce can of white cannellini beans and ½ cup of hemp hearts to replace the cashews.

Veggie Sausage Lasagna

This is one of my all-time favorite recipes. Not only does it showcase perfectly how the staple recipes in this book can be used to re-create classic meals, but it is so good! No one would believe that this lasagna is vegan and also oil-free, wheat-free, and sugar-free. Make this one for your family and friends . . . but don't tell them how healthy it is until they're done raving about it.

DIFFICULTY
Easy

MAKES
one
13 x 9-inch
pan

Ingredients

8 ounces lentil or chickpea lasagna noodles (about 270 grams)

5 cups Simple Tomato Sauce (page 41), divided (see notes)

4 cups Easy Cheese Sauce (page 37), divided (see notes)

8 ounces fresh baby spinach

4 cups Veggie Sausage Ground (page 33)

2 cups Wheat-Free Breadcrumbs (page 46)

Notes

Store leftovers in the fridge for 3 days or in the freezer for 1 month.

The tomato sauce recipe makes 4 cups, so you'll want to double it; freeze the rest to have on hand for an easy pasta night.

Easy Cheese Sauce recipe yield is 1½ cups, so you'll need to double the batch.

Directions

① Preheat the oven to 375°F.

② Prepare the lasagna noodles by boiling them until al dente; they will finish cooking while the lasagna bakes. If you're using oven-ready noodles, you can skip this step.

③ Begin by pouring 1½ cups of tomato sauce on the bottom of a 13 x 9-inch pan. Next, add a layer of noodles.

④ Add 2 cups of tomato sauce on top of the noodles and another layer of noodles on top of the sauce.

⑤ Add half the cheese sauce and top with the spinach. Add another layer of noodles.

⑥ Add the layer of Veggie Sausage Ground and top it with another layer of noodles.

⑦ Finally, add the remaining 1½ cups of tomato sauce.

⑧ Cover and bake for 30 to 35 minutes.

⑨ Remove from the oven. Add the remaining cheese sauce and top with breadcrumbs. Bake uncovered for another 10 minutes or until the breadcrumbs are golden brown.

⑩ Allow the lasagna to cool and set for at least 20 minutes before serving.

Teriyaki No-Meatballs

Drawing inspiration from Japanese-style *tsukune* meatballs, this dish transforms the classic recipe into a wholesome vegan delight. These flavor-packed no-meatballs start with HV Veggie Ground (page 30) and are elevated with the bold additions of ginger, garlic, and miso. Paired with vibrant broccoli and bell peppers and served over nutrient-rich quinoa instead of rice, it all comes together beautifully with a savory, healthy vegan Teriyaki Sauce (page 60).

DIFFICULTY
Easy

MAKES
2 generous servings

Ingredients

VEGGIE NO-MEATBALLS

2 tablespoons miso paste
1 tablespoon coconut aminos
2 tablespoons water
4 teaspoons grated fresh ginger
2 garlic cloves, minced
3 cups HV Veggie Ground (page 30)
4 tablespoons whole psyllium husks
3 tablespoons arrowroot powder
2 tablespoons chickpea flour (see notes)

VEGGIES

¼ cup water or vegetable broth or more as needed
1 medium head broccoli, cut into florets
½ red pepper, diced
½ yellow pepper, diced
½ orange pepper, diced
4 cups Teriyaki Sauce (page 60)
3 cups cooked quinoa or millet to serve
Chopped green onions, for garnish (optional)

Directions

1. Preheat the oven to 350°F. Line a baking sheet with parchment paper and set aside.
2. For the veggie no-meatballs, combine the miso paste, coconut aminos, water, ginger, and garlic in a large bowl.
3. Add the HV Veggie Ground to the miso mixture. Add the whole psyllium husks, arrowroot powder, and chickpea flour, and mix to combine.
4. Divide the mixture into 14 to 16 portions and roll into balls. Place the balls on the lined baking sheet. Bake for 20 minutes, or until firm and darkened in color.
5. While the balls are baking, prepare the veggies. Heat a skillet or wok on medium. Pour the water in the hot pan.
6. Add the veggies and stir-fry, adding more liquid as needed to prevent burning. Once the veggies have a few brown spots, add a little more liquid and cover to steam for 3 to 5 minutes, or until the veggies are cooked to your liking. Pour half the teriyaki sauce over the veggies and mix to combine. Remove from the heat.
7. Serve with the quinoa. Top with the veggies and veggie no-meatballs. Add the remaining teriyaki sauce when serving. Garnish with green onions, if using.

Notes

Store leftover balls and veggies separately; they will keep for up to 5 days in the fridge. You can freeze the balls for up to 3 months.

In a pinch, you can replace the chickpea flour with oat flour.

No-Meatloaf

Craving a comforting dish that's both hearty and wholesome? This HV meatloaf delivers all the cozy vibes of the traditional favorite, minus the meat. The base is my nutrient-rich HV Veggie Ground (page 30), with lots of additional savory flavor. This dish is a redefined classic to satisfy the whole family.

DIFFICULTY
Easy

MAKES
one
9 x 5-inch
loaf pan

Ingredients

3 tablespoons ground flaxseed plus 6 tablespoons water (flax egg)

1 cup cooked quinoa

1 cup rolled oats

1½ cups cooked brown lentils

2 garlic cloves

2½ teaspoons thyme

1¼ teaspoons sage

1¼ teaspoons ground cumin

1¼ teaspoons garlic granules

1 teaspoon salt or to taste

3 cups HV Veggie Ground (page 30)

GLAZE

1 (6- to 7-ounce) jar tomato paste (see note)

2 teaspoons apple cider vinegar

3 tablespoons date paste (page 43)

Directions

1. Preheat the oven to 350°F. Line a 9 x 5-inch loaf pan with parchment paper and set aside.
2. Combine the ground flaxseed and water and set aside.
3. Place the quinoa, oats, lentils, garlic, and spices in a food processor. Pulse until the oats are mostly broken-down; you will still see some pieces.
4. Transfer to a large bowl and add the HV Veggie Ground. Mix until combined. Add previously made flax egg. Mix until well combined.
5. Transfer to the parchment-lined loaf pan and smooth the top. Bake for 25 minutes.
6. While the loaf is baking, mix the glaze ingredients in a small bowl.
7. Remove the loaf and top it with the glaze. Bake for an additional 15 to 20 minutes, or until the glaze has darkened and looks caramelized.
8. Allow the loaf to cool for 10 minutes. Remove from the pan, cut, and serve with a side of cauliflower mash, cooked vegetables, and/or a salad.

Note

Since tomatoes are acidic and can have a reaction with the metal in cans, I prefer to purchase my tomato paste in a glass jar.

Burger and Ranch Pizza

Pizza is rarely considered healthy food, but this recipe is about to change that! With its soft cauliflower crust it's perfect for any topping, but here I'm going classic: tomato sauce (page 41), with a generous layer of veggie ground (page 30), and finishing it off with a drizzle of creamy dill ranch (page 65). This is a great base, so add your choice of toppings and make it your own!

DIFFICULTY
Medium

MAKES
one 12-inch pizza

Ingredients

CRUST

4 cups cauliflower florets (about ½ large head of cauliflower)

2½ tablespoons ground flaxseed or ground chia seeds

¼ cup cold water

⅓ cup almond flour or oat flour

1 teaspoon Italian seasoning

½ teaspoon garlic granules

½ teaspoon salt or to taste

TOPPINGS

1 cup (or more if you're a sauce lover!) Simple Tomato Sauce (page 41)

HV Veggie Ground (page 30)

½ pint cherry tomatoes, halved, or 1 medium tomato, chopped

½ red onion, sliced thinly

¼ cup Creamy Dill Ranch Dressing (page 65)

Chopped green onions, for garnish (optional)

Directions

1. Preheat the oven to 450°F. Line two baking sheets with parchment paper.

2. Cut the cauliflower into small florets. Steam the florets for 5 to 7 minutes, or until they are soft and fall apart. Make sure they still hold together but can easily be pulled apart. Set aside.

3. Combine the ground flaxseed and cold water and set aside to thicken.

4. Combine the remaining crust ingredients in a bowl.

5. Once the cauliflower florets have cooled enough to handle, place them in a nut milk bag or cheesecloth. Gather the sides of the cheesecloth at the top and tightly twist and squeeze to drain the water. Continue this process until the cauliflower is as dry as possible. You will be left with a ball of mashed cauliflower.

6. Add the strained cauliflower to the remaining crust ingredients and mix well. The consistency will be soft but can easily hold together to form a ball.

7. Place the ball onto a piece of parchment paper. Place another sheet of parchment paper on top and roll until ¼ inch thick and about 12 inches in diameter. Alternatively, press the ball with your hands to form a disk shape. Using your hands, you can form a raised edge around the pizza.

(recipe continues)

Burger and Ranch Pizza (continued)

⑧ Transfer the crust to the parchment-lined baking sheet and bake for 18 to 22 minutes, or until lightly browned. Remove from the oven.

⑨ Spread the tomato sauce over the crust. Top the pizza with the veggie ground, cherry tomatoes, and red onions.

⑩ Bake the pizza for an additional 8 to 10 minutes.

⑪ Drizzle with creamy dill ranch and garnish with green onions, if using.

Sweet Potato Shepherd's Pie

Creamy potatoes, veggie ground, and a rich crust all bring to mind a classic shepherd's pie. This recipe covers all the bases but with healthy twists: With my HV Veggie Ground (page 30), a healthier sweet potato mash topping, and a protein-rich almond-based crust, this shepherd's pie is as satisfying as it is nourishing. Perfect for a cozy family dinner, this dish is also great for meal prep; double the batch and freeze one for later!

DIFFICULTY
Easy

MAKES
one 9-inch pie pan or 7-inch springform pan

Ingredients

CRUST

2 tablespoons ground flaxseed plus 5 tablespoons water (flax egg)

1¼ cups almond flour

⅓ cup arrowroot powder

¼ teaspoon baking powder

¼ teaspoon salt or to taste

SWEET POTATO MASH

4 small sweet potatoes (see notes)

½ cup cashew cream (see notes)

4 tablespoons chopped chives, plus extra for garnish

2 tablespoons nutritional yeast

1 teaspoon salt or to taste

¼ teaspoon black pepper

3 cups HV Veggie Ground (page 30)

½ cup Easy Cheese Sauce (page 37)

Directions

① Combine the ground flaxseed and water and set aside.

② In a large bowl, combine the almond flour, arrowroot powder, baking powder, and salt.

③ Add the flax egg and mix with a spoon until it begins to come together. Use your hands to bring the mixture together and form a ball of dough.

④ Place the ball of dough between two sheets of parchment paper to roll. Roll to fit a 9-inch pie pan.

⑤ Place the rolled crust in the pan and press to line the pan. Trim excess dough from the edges of the pan.

⑥ Poke the crust with a fork, cover, and place it in the freezer for 20 minutes. In the meantime, preheat the oven to 400°F.

⑦ Remove the piecrust from the freezer. Cover the piecrust with parchment and use pie weights or other heat-safe material to weigh the crust down. Parbake for 15 minutes.

⑧ Place the sweet potatoes onto a parchment-lined baking sheet. Poke holes in them with a fork. Bake at 400°F for 40 minutes, or until a fork inserts with ease. Reduce the oven temperature to 350°F.

(recipe continues)

Sweet Potato Shepherd's Pie (continued)

(9) Once the potatoes are cooled, place them in a bowl and mash them with a potato masher or fork. Add the cashew cream, chives, nutritional yeast, salt, and black pepper. Mix or mash to combine.

(10) Add the HV Veggie Ground to the parbaked piecrust. Top with sweet potato mash.

(11) Bake for 20 minutes, or until the crust is golden on the edges.

(12) Drizzle with cheese sauce and garnish with additional chives.

Notes

Leftovers will keep in the fridge for 3 days and in the freezer for up to 3 months.

Sweet potatoes are my go-to, but feel free to use your favorite variety of potato.

Although baking sweet potatoes gives a sweeter and slightly more flavorful result, boiling or steaming sweet potatoes generally results in a lower glycemic index, leading to a slower and more gradual rise in blood sugar levels.

For cashew cream, blend 1/4 cup of soaked cashews with 1/2 cup of water.

Notes

Leftovers will keep for 3 days in the fridge. Freeze a whole pan or individual portions for 1 month.

Check your local health-food store for oil-free organic sprouted corn tortillas.

No-Chick'n Enchilada Casserole

Think of this casserole as an "enchilasagna"—a mouthwatering combo of two classics. Organic corn tortillas replace traditional noodles while enchilada sauce takes the place of tomato sauce for a flavorful punch. Packed with layers of hearty beans and vibrant vegetables and topped with rich and creamy Easy Cheese Sauce (page 37), this dish is the best of both worlds.

DIFFICULTY
Medium

MAKES
one 13 x 9-inch casserole pan

Ingredients

ENCHILADA SAUCE

3 tablespoons ground chili powder
3 teaspoons ground cumin
1½ teaspoons garlic powder
1½ teaspoons dried oregano
Ground black pepper to taste
1½ teaspoons salt or to taste
½ teaspoon ground cinnamon
⅓ cup tomato paste
7 cups vegetable broth
3 teaspoons apple cider vinegar

CASSEROLE

1 red pepper, diced
½ red onion, diced
1 zucchini, diced
4 cups Chick'n-Style Mushrooms with Mexican-style seasoning (page 34)
18 (6-inch) or 12 (9-inch) organic sprouted corn tortillas (see notes)
1½ cups cooked black beans, or 1 (15-ounce) can black beans
2 cups Easy Cheese Sauce, divided (page 37)

Directions

1. Preheat the oven to 350°F.
2. In a saucepan, whisk together the spices, tomato paste, broth, and apple cider vinegar. Allow to simmer over medium heat for 10 minutes, or until the sauce is reduced and thickened. Remove from the heat. You'll be using this in thirds.
3. For the casserole, in a large bowl, place the veggies and mushrooms; toss to combine.
4. Put a small amount of the enchilada sauce in the bottom of a 13 x 9-inch pan, just enough to coat.
5. Overlap 6 small or 2 to 3 large tortillas to create a layer. Cover the tortillas with half the veggie mix and the beans.
6. Add one-third of the enchilada sauce and about ¾ cup of cheese sauce. Cover with another layer of 6 small or 2 to 3 large tortillas.
7. Top with the remaining veggie mix; then cover with another third of the enchilada sauce and about ¾ cup of cheese sauce.
8. Finally, top with one last layer of tortillas and the last of the enchilada sauce and cheese sauce.
9. Bake covered for 20 minutes; then uncover and bake for another 10 minutes, or until the vegetables are cooked.

Jamaican-Style Sweet Potato and Chickpea Curry

Not only is curry powder delicious, with ingredients such as turmeric, but it has health benefits too. This recipe has additional turmeric, as well as allspice and thyme, which adds a Jamaican flavor profile. Combined with chickpeas and sweet potatoes, this dish is quick to make, full of flavor, and perfect for a comforting, satisfying meal.

DIFFICULTY
Easy

MAKES
4 servings

Ingredients

- 3–4 cups oil-free, salt-free vegetable broth or water, divided
- 1 small yellow onion, diced
- 3 garlic cloves, minced
- 1 jalapeño, stemmed and minced (see notes)
- 2½ tablespoons curry powder
- 1 teaspoon ground allspice
- 1 teaspoon dried thyme
- ½ teaspoon ground turmeric
- 2 teaspoons salt or to taste
- 6 medium sweet potatoes, chopped into 2-inch cubes
- 2⅔ cups cooked chickpeas, or 2 (15-ounce) cans chickpeas, drained and rinsed
- 3 cups cooked millet or quinoa, for serving

Directions

1. Heat a large saucepan on medium. Pour ¼ cup of vegetable broth in the pan.
2. When the broth begins to simmer, add the onions and sauté for 2 to 3 minutes; then add the garlic and jalapeño. Sauté for an additional 2 to 3 minutes. Add extra broth as necessary.
3. Add the dry spices and salt. Sauté momentarily. Add the sweet potatoes and chickpeas. Mix to coat potatoes in the spices.
4. Add 2 cups of the broth. Cover and simmer for 15 to 20 minutes, or until the potatoes are soft and breaking slightly (do not overcook).
5. You can add more liquid in small amounts if necessary. As the potatoes break down slightly, the sauce will thicken. Sweet potatoes cook quicker than white potatoes, so take care not to overcook them. You want them to be well cooked but still have substance. This curry should be thick and saucy.
6. Allow to sit and thicken slightly before eating. Serve with a side of millet.

Notes

Store leftovers in the fridge for 3 to 5 days or in the freezer for up to 3 months.

If you are heat sensitive, you'll want to remove the seeds from the jalapeño before dicing.

Jamaican curries often have coconut milk added. I limit coconut milk in my recipes due to the saturated fat content; however, if coconut milk is an ingredient you enjoy, you can add up to ¾ of a cup in the final 5 minutes of cooking.

Mushroom Kebabs with Pineapple Jalapeño Sauce

These kebabs are perfect year-round, but they truly shine in the summer, paired with a salad like my Sweet Dijon Pasta Salad (page 171). What sets them apart is the irresistible sweet and spicy pineapple jalapeño sauce, which comes together effortlessly in a blender. With just a quick prep of veggies and mushrooms on skewers, you'll have a simple yet showstopping dish ready in no time!

DIFFICULTY
Easy

MAKES
2 generous servings

Ingredients

SAUCE

- 2 cups chopped fresh pineapple (see notes)
- 2 jalapeños, stemmed and seeded
- 4 garlic cloves
- 4 tablespoons coconut aminos
- 1 teaspoon smoked paprika
- ¼ teaspoon smoked chipotle or to taste

VEGETABLES

- ½ red pepper, diced
- ½ yellow pepper, diced
- ½ orange pepper, diced
- 2 medium zucchinis, halved and cut into ½-inch pieces
- 1 red onion, cut into 2-inch chunks
- 1 pound lion's mane or oyster mushrooms, broken into large pieces
- 3 cups cooked quinoa, for serving

Directions

1. If you are using wooden skewers, soak them in water for about 30 minutes before using (to prevent burning). Preheat the oven to 400°F. Line a baking sheet with parchment paper and set aside.
2. Prepare the sauce by combining all the sauce ingredients in a high-speed blender, and blend until smooth.
3. Arrange the vegetables and mushrooms on the skewers.
4. Place the skewers on a parchment-lined baking sheet. Brush generously with the sauce. Sprinkle the kebabs with smoked chipotle seasoning.
5. Bake for 20 to 30 minutes, or until the vegetables are tender.
6. Serve on a bed of quinoa. Top with extra sauce and chipotle seasoning if desired.

Notes

Cooked kebabs will keep for 3 days in the fridge.

If you use canned pineapple, make sure to choose a brand with no added sugars. Give it a quick rinse before using in the recipe.

Taco-Style Cauliflower Stuffed Sweet Potato

Sweet potatoes are a go-to for many people who are exploring healthy vegan eating—and with good reason. They are high in potassium, magnesium, and fiber, as well as other beneficial nutrients. But beyond that, they just taste good and lend themselves to a range of recipes. The first time I made these stuffed sweet potatoes, I was genuinely amazed at how delicious they turned out. While the naturally sweet and creamy sweet potato makes for a delicious base, the flavor-packed roasted cauliflower and sweet and tangy Jalapeño Lime Sauce (page 60) steal the show here!

DIFFICULTY
Easy

MAKES
4 servings

Ingredients

4 small sweet potatoes

TACO-STYLE CAULIFLOWER

1 medium head of cauliflower, cut into florets

1 red onion, sliced

3 teaspoons dried oregano

3 teaspoons smoked paprika

3 teaspoons garlic granules

1½ teaspoons onion granules

Cayenne pepper to taste

6 tablespoons coconut aminos

TOPPINGS

1 cup cooked black beans

1 avocado, mashed

Jalapeño Lime Sauce (page 60)

Directions

1. Preheat the oven to 400°F. Line a baking sheet with parchment paper.

2. Cut the sweet potatoes in half lengthwise. Place them cut side down on the parchment-lined baking sheet and bake for 20 minutes, or until they are soft. Remove from the oven. Adjust the oven temperature to 425°F.

3. In a large bowl, combine the cauliflower florets, red onion, seasonings, and coconut aminos. Spread the mixture evenly on the parchment-lined baking sheet.

4. Bake for 20 minutes, mix, and bake for an additional 20 minutes. Remove from the oven.

5. Transfer the baked sweet potatoes to a plate and add the taco-style cauliflower. Top with black beans, avocado, and Jalapeño Lime Sauce.

Note

The cauliflower mix will keep in the fridge for 3 days, as will the sweet potatoes (I recommend storing them separately).

Palak "Paneer"

I love the flavors of the classic Indian dish, *palak paneer*. *Palak* translates to "spinach," while *paneer* refers to a fresh cheese. In my HV spin, I've kept the rich spinach base and aromatic seasonings, but I swap the paneer with a homemade alternative to tofu that is made using pumpkin seeds (page 23), or you could use tofu.

DIFFICULTY
Medium

MAKES
2 generous servings

Ingredients

PANEER

15 ounces tofu or pumfu (page 23)

2 tablespoons coconut aminos

1 tablespoon nutritional yeast

¼ teaspoon garam masala

SPINACH

7–8 cups chopped packed spinach (see notes)

⅓ cup cashews, soaked for at least 2 hours

1 garlic clove

1-inch piece fresh ginger root

GRAVY

¼ cup water

1 medium onion, diced

2 garlic cloves, minced

1 serrano chili, minced

2 medium tomatoes, diced

1½ teaspoons ground cumin

1 bay leaf

¼ teaspoon ground turmeric

½ teaspoon sweet paprika

½ teaspoon garam masala

¼ cup cashew cream (see notes)

Salt to taste

Directions

(1) Preheat the oven to 400°F. Line a baking sheet with parchment paper.

(2) Cut tofu into 1-inch cubes and place them in a medium bowl along with the coconut aminos, nutritional yeast, and garam masala. Toss until coated and pour onto the prepared baking sheet. Bake for 20 minutes, flipping halfway through cooking.

(3) Fill a medium bowl with ice water and set aside. Bring a medium pot of water to boil. Blanch the spinach by adding it to the boiling water and removing it as soon as the leaves are wilted, in about 30 seconds. Immediately transfer to ice water to stop the cooking process. Transfer to a colander; drain and set aside.

(4) Place the spinach in a blender with drained cashews, garlic, and ginger and blend until smooth.

(5) For the gravy, in a large skillet or pan over medium-high heat, add the water, onions, garlic, and chili. Allow to cook for 3 to 5 minutes, or until softened. Add water as necessary to prevent sticking.

(6) Add the tomatoes and cook for 3 to 5 minutes. Add the cumin, bay leaf, turmeric, and paprika. Continue to cook for 5 to 7 minutes, or until the tomatoes have broken down and the mixture is thickened.

(recipe continues)

Palak "Paneer" (continued)

⑦ Add the puréed spinach and garam masala. Mix to combine. Add the tofu, cashew cream, and salt. Mix to combine. Serve with millet, quinoa, or bread of choice.

Notes

Leftovers will keep for 3 to 5 days in the fridge.

Use 12 ounces of frozen spinach. Thaw and squeeze to remove excess water.

Cashew cream can be made by blending 1⁄4 cup of soaked raw cashews with 1⁄2 cup of water until smooth.

You can easily turn this dish into another Indian dish, *palak aloo*, by swapping the tofu for potatoes. Just steam your diced potatoes until they are cooked but firm and add them in the last couple of minutes of step 5.

Jamaican Patties

If you haven't experienced Jamaican patties yet, get ready! Known for their golden crust and boldly spiced filling, these iconic Caribbean hand pies have earned fans worldwide. In this recipe, I'm putting my HV twist on the classic by using a nutty almond crust and a beautifully seasoned HV Veggie Ground filling (page 30) instead of the more typical ground beef. The result? A p ant-based take on a timeless favorite that'll have you going back for more.

DIFFICULTY
Medium

MAKES
6 patties

Ingredients

FILLING

½ yellow onion, minced

1 garlic clove, minced

½ Scotch bonnet pepper, or to taste (optional)

3 cups HV Veggie Ground (page 30)

2 teaspoons curry powder

1 teaspoon ground allspice

1 teaspoon dried thyme

1 tablespoon ground flaxseed

½ teaspoon salt or to taste

CRUST

4 tablespoons ground flaxseed plus ½ cup plus 2 tablespoons water (flax egg)

2½ cups almond flour

⅔ cup arrowroot powder

¼ teaspoon baking powder

¼ teaspoon ground turmeric

1 teaspoon salt or to taste

Directions

① Place the onion, garlic, and Scotch bonnet pepper (if using) in a medium skillet. Add in a small amount of water and sauté over medium heat until soft and the water has evaporated, in 3 to 5 minutes. Set aside.

② In a large bowl, place the veggie grounc, sautéed onions and garlic, spices, ground flaxseed, and salt and mix to combine.

③ Combine the ground flaxseed and water and set aside.

④ In a large bowl, combine the almond flcur, arrowroot powder, baking powder, turmeric, and salt.

⑤ Add the flax egg and mix with a spoon until it begins to come together. It is best to use your hands at this point to bring it all together to form a ball of dough.

⑥ Divide the dough into 6 equal portions and roll into balls.

⑦ One at a time, place each ball of dough between two sheets of parchment paper and roll it into a roughly 8-inch circle. Use a 7-inch or 8-inch round bowl or other round object and cut around it to create a clean edge.

⑧ Add about ⅓ cup of filling (adjust if necessary) to one half of the circular crust. Dip your finger into some water and run it along the edge of the circle that has the filling.

(recipe continues)

Jamaican Patties (continued)

⑨ Gently fold over the crust's other side, taking care not to tear it. This dough will not stretch like regular dough. Seal the pocket by gently pressing with a fork. Dip the fork in a small amount of water if it is sticking.

⑩ Place the covered patties in the freezer for 20 minutes.

⑪ Preheat the oven to 350°F.

⑫ Poke tops with a fork several times. Bake for 20 to 25 minutes, until the crusts are lightly golden around the edges.

Note

Patties will keep in the fridge for 3 days. You can freeze them before or after baking for up to 3 months. Thaw and bake or reheat in the oven.

DESSERTS

Probably the biggest pitfall for people who desire to eat a healthy diet is desserts. Healthy vegan eating doesn't mean giving up sweets. In fact, healthy desserts are one of my specialties, and I have received thousands of messages from people who are elated that I have created delicious desserts free of refined sugar, wheat, or oil. In this section you'll find some of my favorite cakes, cookies, pies, puddings, and more, all made with healthy flours, nut butters, and, of course, dates. The best part? They taste amazing. I can say with total confidence that my HV desserts will blow you away!

Peanut Butter Cups

I used to love Reese's Peanut Butter Cups but hadn't indulged in them for years—until I discovered how surprisingly easy it is to make my own with just a few simple ingredients!

DIFFICULTY
Medium

MAKES
12 cups

Ingredients

3/4 cup peanut butter (see notes)

3/4 cup date paste (page 43)

2 teaspoons vanilla extract

1/2 teaspoon salt or to taste (optional)

12 ounces date-sweetened or unsweetened chocolate (see notes)

Notes

Store these chocolates in an airtight container in the refrigerator or freezer. Remove and thaw when in need of a treat.

Choose a nut butter without any added oils or sweetener.

You can use chocolate chips or a chopped chocolate bar.

Directions

(1) Line a cupcake tin with silicone or paper liners and set aside. You can also just use silicone liners.

(2) Combine the peanut butter, date paste, vanilla extract, and salt, if using, in a medium bowl. Set in the fridge while melting the chocolate.

(3) To melt the chocolate, create a double boiler: Pour 2 cups of water in a small pot. Place a glass bowl or stainless-steel pot on top. Set the burner to medium-low heat. Place the chocolate in the bowl and mix while it melts. Continue to stir the chocolate until it is completely melted and smooth. Turn off the burner. Take care to handle the bowl with care: It will be hot! (You can also microwave the chocolate to melt it.)

(4) Pour in 1 to 2 teaspoons of melted chocolate to cover the bottom of the liners.

(5) Remove the peanut butter mixture from the fridge. Roll 1 to 1½ tablespoons of peanut butter into a ball and gently flatten into a disk shape. Place the disk on top of the chocolate in the silicone liner. The closer the disk is to the edge of the liner, the thinner the chocolate will be.

(6) Using a ladle or measuring cup, pour just enough melted chocolate to cover the height of the filling. Repeat this process for all the chocolates.

(7) Refrigerate for 30 minutes or more until the chocolate is solid.

Simple Chocolate Turtles

Whether you're a longtime fan of chocolate turtles or discovering them for the first time, you'll love this healthier twist on the classic treat. With a simple yet sophisticated blend of pecans, date caramel, and chocolate, these bites are perfect for satisfying a quick sweet craving or sharing as a thoughtful gift.

DIFFICULTY
Medium

MAKES
12 turtles

Ingredients

2 cups raw pecans

1 cup date paste (page 43)

2 teaspoons vanilla extract

⅛ teaspoon salt or to taste

12 ounces date-sweetened or unsweetened chocolate (see notes)

Notes

Store these chocolates in an airtight container in the refrigerator or freezer. Remove and thaw when in need of a treat.

You can use chocolate chips or a chopped chocolate bar.

Directions

1. Preheat the oven to 350°F. Line a baking sheet with parchment paper.
2. Spread pecans evenly on the parchment-lined baking sheet. Roast the pecans for 10 to 15 minutes, or until aromatic. Check them halfway through baking time as nuts can burn easily. Roasting the pecans is optional; they can also be used raw. When done, transfer to a bowl.
3. To make date caramel, combine the date paste, vanilla extract, and salt in a small saucepan and cook on low-medium heat until the caramel thickens and darkens slightly, in 5 to 7 minutes. Stir continuously to avoid burning.
4. To melt the chocolate, create a double boiler: Pour 2 cups of water in a small pot. Place a glass bowl or stainless-steel pot on top. Set the burner to medium-low heat. Place the chocolate in the bowl and mix while it melts. Continue to stir the chocolate until it is completely melted and smooth. Turn off the burner. Take care to handle the bowl with care: It will be hot! (You can also microwave the chocolate to melt it.)
5. Use half the melted chocolate to form the base of the turtles. Pour 2 teaspoons of melted chocolate onto the parchment-lined baking sheet to create 12 circles.
6. Place 3 to 4 pecans on top of each circle of chocolate. Refrigerate for 5 to 10 minutes to set.

(recipe continues)

Simple Chocolate Turtles (continued)

(7) Remove the pecan bases from the refrigerator and add a heaping teaspoon of date caramel on top.

(8) Transfer the chocolate turtles to a cooling rack. Place another baking sheet under the rack to catch any excess chocolate.

(9) Heat the remaining chocolate if it's hardening. Heat it just until liquid; if it is too hot, it will melt the base chocolate.

(10) Using a measuring cup or ladle, pour chocolate over the top of each turtle. Make sure the chocolate has fully coated each one.

(11) Allow the turtles to set on the counter or in the fridge.

Strawberry-Fig Cookies

First introduced in 1891, Fig Newtons were among the earliest commercially produced baked goods in the United States, and they remain a much-loved classic to this day. This healthier twist captures the nostalgia with a familiar, soft, tender cookie filled with a sweet strawberry-fig jam. I use almond flour and nut butter for the dough, which makes these treats a wholesome snack with a protein boost.

DIFFICULTY
Medium

MAKES
15 cookies

Ingredients

FILLING

½ cup chopped dried figs

16 ounces fresh or frozen strawberries

1 teaspoon vanilla extract

½ cup water

DOUGH

1¼ cups almond flour

1 cup oat flour

2 teaspoons baking powder

½ cup date paste (page 43)

1 teaspoon vanilla extract

¼ cup plus 2 tablespoons nut butter (see notes)

Pinch of salt

Notes

Store these cookies in an airtight container in the fridge for up to 5 days; they are even better the next day! They can also be stored in the freezer for up to 1 month.

Choose a nut butter without any added oils or sweetener.

Directions

① Combine the filling ingredients in a medium-size saucepan and simmer over medium-low heat until the mixture is very thick. This can take over 1 hour. The thicker the filling is, the easier it will be to assemble the cookies. Remove from the heat and set aside to cool completely.

② Preheat the oven to 350°F. Line a baking sheet with parchment paper and set aside.

③ Prepare the dough by placing the almond flour, oat flour, and baking powder in a large bowl. Mix to combine.

④ In a separate small bowl, place the date paste, vanilla extract, nut butter, and salt. Mix well until combined.

⑤ Combine the wet and dry ingredients until a dough forms.

⑥ Place the dough on parchment paper. Place another sheet of parchment paper on top and roll it into a rectangle approximately 10 x 15 inches. It should be about ⅛ to ¼ inch thick.

⑦ Cut this rectangle down the middle to create 2 rectangles approximately 5 x 15 inches.

⑧ Put the cooled filling in a food processor and process until smooth.

(recipe continues)

Strawberry-Fig Cookies (continued)

⑨ Add half the filling vertically down the center of each rectangle.

⑩ Using the parchment paper, gently lift and bring each side of the dough together, allowing the sides to overlap slightly, creating a roll. Next, using the parchment paper, gently turn the roll over so the seam is under the roll.

⑪ Using a sharp knife, cut the roll into cookies that are 1½ to 2 inches thick. Place them on the parchment-lined baking sheet.

⑫ Bake for 10 to 12 minutes. Allow to cool.

Chewy Chocolate Chip Cookies

Chocolate chip cookies may seem basic to some, but there's a reason they are one of America's favorite treats! My HV twist on this classic is just as irresistible as the original and even easier to whip up. With a nut butter base and date sweetener, they are perfectly sweet, simple, and satisfying. For a little extra flavor, try adding cinnamon to the mix.

DIFFICULTY
Easy

MAKES
12 cookies

Ingredients

½ cup date paste (page 43)

¼ cup nut or seed butter (see notes)

½ teaspoon vanilla extract

1½ cups almond flour

½ teaspoon baking soda

Pinch of salt

¼–⅓ cup date-sweetened chocolate chips

Notes

Store in the fridge for up to 5 days or in the freezer for up to 1 month

Choose a nut butter without any added oils or sweetener.

Directions

1. Preheat the oven to 350°F. Line a baking sheet with parchment paper and set aside.
2. Place the date paste, nut or seed butter, and vanilla extract in a large bowl and mix well.
3. In a separate large bowl, combine the almond flour, baking soda, and salt.
4. Add the dry mixture to the wet mixture. Mix until a dough is formed.
5. Fold in the chocolate chips.
6. Divide the dough into 12 equal portions and roll into balls. Place them on the parchment-lined baking sheet.
7. Using the bottom of a cup and a piece of parchment paper, flatten the balls to ½ inch thick.
8. Bake for 10 to 12 minutes, or until lightly golden on the edges.

Sesame Date Cookies

This recipe is inspired by dates and tahini, two classic ingredients found in many Middle Eastern desserts. Sesame seeds are among the richest plant-based sources of calcium, and when paired with the warm, aromatic notes of cardamom, they create a subtly sweet, nutty, and chewy harmony that's both comforting and nutrient rich.

DIFFICULTY
Easy

MAKES
12 cookies

Ingredients

½ cup date paste (page 43)
¼ cup tahini (runny is best)
1½ cups almond flour
½ teaspoon baking soda
¼ teaspoon ground cardamom
Pinch of salt
⅓ cup sesame seeds

Notes

Store in the fridge for up to 5 days or in the freezer for up to 1 month.

NUT-FREE: Replace the almond flour with tiger nut flour.

Directions

1. Preheat the oven to 350°F. Line a baking sheet with parchment paper and set aside.
2. Combine the date paste and tahini in a large bowl.
3. In a separate large bowl, combine the almond flour, baking soda, cardamom, and salt.
4. Add the dry mixture to the wet mixture. Mix until a dough is formed.
5. Divide the dough into 12 equal portions and roll into balls.
6. Pour the sesame seeds into a small bowl or onto a plate. Roll the balls in the sesame seeds to coat them completely and place them on the parchment-lined baking sheet.
7. Using the bottom of a cup and a piece of parchment paper, flatten the balls to about ½ inch thick.
8. Bake for 8 to 10 minutes, or until the sesame seeds are slightly golden.

Cherry Pistachio Cookies

Pistachios are hands down one of my favorite nuts, and these cookies are a true celebration of their flavor. Paired with dried cherries, they create a deliciously unique treat that is slightly tart and not overwhelmingly sweet, with a perfect chewy-crumbly texture.

DIFFICULTY
Easy

MAKES
12 cookies

Ingredients

¾ cup shelled and ground pistachios, divided

½ cup date paste (page 43)

¼ cup nut butter (see notes)

¼ teaspoon almond extract

½ teaspoon vanilla extract

1 cup almond flour

½ teaspoon baking soda

Pinch of salt (optional)

½ cup sugar-free dried cherries

Notes

Store in the fridge for up to 3 days or in the freezer for up to 1 month.

Choose a nut butter without any added oils or sweetener.

Directions

1. Preheat the oven to 350°F. Line a baking sheet with parchment paper and set aside.
2. Grind the pistachios in a food processor, blender, or coffee/seed grinder until a fine crumb is achieved. They do not have to be as finely ground as almond flour; be careful not to overgrind.
3. Combine the date paste, nut butter, almond extract, and vanilla extract in a large bowl.
4. In a separate large bowl, combine the almond flour, ½ cup of the ground pistachios, baking soda, and salt, if using.
5. Add the dry mixture to the wet mixture. Mix until a dough is formed.
6. Fold in the dried cherries.
7. Divide the dough into 12 equal portions and roll into balls.
8. Pour the remaining ¼ cup of ground pistachios into a small bowl or onto a plate. Roll the balls in the ground pistachios to coat them completely and place them on the parchment-lined baking sheet.
9. Using the bottom of a cup and a piece of parchment paper, flatten the balls to about ½ inch thick.
10. Bake for 10 to 12 minutes.

Peanut Butter Chocolate Chip Cookies

Chickpeas are my secret weapon for so many desserts. Not only are they packed with impressive health benefits, but they also seamlessly blend into recipes. Here, their nuttiness complements the peanut butter and also offsets the sweetness for a perfect balance.

DIFFICULTY
Easy

MAKES
12–14 cookies

Ingredients

1⅓ cups cooked chickpeas, or 1 (15-ounce) can chickpeas, drained and rinsed

½ cup plant milk

12 large Medjool dates, pitted

1 teaspoon vanilla extract

Pinch of salt

½ cup peanut butter (see notes)

½ teaspoon baking soda

½ teaspoon baking powder

¾ cup date-sweetened chocolate chips

Directions

1. Preheat the oven to 350°F. Line a large baking sheet with parchment paper and set aside.
2. Place the chickpeas, plant milk, dates, vanilla extract, and salt in a food processor and process until completely smooth.
3. Add the peanut butter and continue to blend.
4. Once the ingredients are well combined and smooth, add the baking soda and powder and blend briefly, just until combined. The dough will resemble a thick batter.
5. Stir in the chocolate chips. You can do this directly in the food processor or transfer the mixture to a bowl.
6. Use a 2- to 3-tablespoon cookie scoop to scoop and shape 12 to 14 cookies 2 inches apart on the baking sheet.
7. Using the back of a clean spoon, evenly flatten the cookies to ¼ to ½ inch thick. It is helpful to wet the spoon for this step to prevent the cookie batter from sticking.
8. Bake for 18 to 20 minutes. Let cool on the baking sheet until just warm before transferring to a cooling rack.

Notes

These will keep in the fridge for up to 3 days. I actually prefer them after they've been in the fridge!

If you are avoiding peanuts, this recipe can be made with any nut or seed butter.

Choose a nut butter without any added oils or sweetener.

Oatmeal Raisin Cookies

Raisins can be a love-it-or-leave-it ingredient, but I love them, especially in oatmeal raisin cookies, one of my all-time favorites. If you're a fellow fan, this recipe is a must-try. Made with chickpeas instead of flour, it's a wholesome and delicious take on the classic cookie. If you are nut-free or want to try something new, use tahini in place of the nut butter.

DIFFICULTY
Easy

MAKES
12 cookies

Ingredients

1⅓ cups cooked chickpeas, or 1 (15-ounce) can chickpeas, drained and rinsed

¾ cup plant milk

12 large Medjool dates, pitted

1 teaspoon vanilla extract

Pinch of salt

½ cup nut or seed butter (see notes)

½ teaspoon baking soda

½ teaspoon baking powder

1¼ cups rolled oats

¾ cup raisins

Notes

These will keep in the fridge for up to 5 days.

Choose a nut butter without any added oils or sweetener.

NUT-FREE: Replace the nut butter with tahini.

Directions

1. Preheat the oven to 350°F. Line a large baking sheet with parchment paper and set aside.
2. Place the chickpeas, plant milk, dates, vanilla extract, and salt in a food processor and process until smooth.
3. Add the nut butter and continue to blend.
4. Once the ingredients are well combined and smooth, add the baking soda and baking powder and blend briefly, just until combined.
5. Add the oats and pulse to combine.
6. Stir in the raisins. You can do this in the food processor or transfer the mixture to a bowl.
7. Use a 2- to 3-tablespoon cookie scoop to scoop and shape 12 cookies 2 inches apart on the baking sheet.
8. Using the back of a clean spoon, evenly flatten the cookies to ½ inch thick. It is helpful to wet the spoon for this step to prevent the cookie batter from sticking.
9. Bake for 12 to 15 minutes. Let cool on the baking sheet until just warm before transferring to a cooling rack.

Brownie Cookies

These brownie cookies might surprise you with a secret ingredient, one of my favorites—sweet potatoes! While you'd never guess they're in there, the sweet potatoes give these cookies their moist and fudgy texture. Best of all, they're easy to make and come together quickly in a food processor.

DIFFICULTY
Easy

MAKES
12 cookies

Ingredients

1½ cups mashed sweet potato, or about 2 small to medium potatoes

½ cup nut or seed butter (see notes)

¼ cup cocoa powder

⅓ cup date paste (page 43)

1½ teaspoons baking powder

1 teaspoon vanilla extract

3 tablespoons coconut flour

Pinch of salt

3 tablespoons plant milk or as needed

⅓–⅔ cup walnuts or date-sweetened chocolate chips (optional)

Directions

1. Preheat the oven to 350°F. Line a large baking sheet with parchment paper and set aside.
2. Place all the ingredients in a food processor, except the plant milk and the walnuts, if using. Process until well combined. Add small amounts of the plant milk if the mixture is too thick to blend. Cookie dough should be scoopable but not dry.
3. Transfer the dough to a bowl and, if using, fold in the walnuts.
4. Use a 2- to 3-tablespoon cookie scoop to scoop 12 cookies 2 inches apart on the baking sheet.
5. Gently press the cookies or leave mounded for a domed shape. If leaving dome-shaped, the center will be more fudgy.
6. Bake for 15 to 18 minutes, or until the cookies are slightly firm to the touch. Let cool on the baking sheet until just warm before transferring to a cooling rack.

Notes

These will keep in the fridge for up to 3 days.

Choose a nut or seed butter without any added oils or sweetener.

NUT-FREE: Replace the walnuts with chocolate chips and use tahini to replace the nut butter.

Chocolate Chip Cookie Dough

Who says cookie dough is just for kids? Chock-full of nutrients, this quick and easy recipe is a sweet, energizing midday treat that won't give you a sugar crash. It's the ultimate fix for sweet cravings, and both kids and adults can enjoy making and eating this treat!

DIFFICULTY
Easy

MAKES
2 servings

Ingredients

1⅓ cups cooked chickpeas, or 1 (15-ounce) can chickpeas, drained and rinsed

2 tablespoons nut butter (see notes)

½ cup almond flour

4 Medjool dates, pitted

1 teaspoon vanilla extract

1–2 tablespoons plant milk as needed

¼ cup date-sweetened chocolate chips

Directions

1. Combine all the ingredients except the chocolate chips in a food processor or blender and blend until completely smooth.
2. Transfer to a bowl. Mix in the chocolate chips.

Notes

Store in an airtight container in the fridge for 3 days. This will also keep in the freezer for 1 month (for freezing, portion out into individual balls). Thaw when ready to enjoy.

Choose a nut butter without any added oils or sweetener.

NUT-FREE: Replace the almond flour with tiger nut flour. Replace the nut butter with tahini.

Double-Chocolate No-Bake Brownies

While the idea of not baking a brownie may not seem to make sense, trust me, it's what makes these brownies extra decadent. The chewy, nutty base comes together easily in the food processor, but the real treat here is the luscious, melt-in-your-mouth ganache.

DIFFICULTY
Easy

MAKES
16 squares

Ingredients

BROWNIE BASE

2 cups walnuts

18 Medjool dates, pitted

⅔ cup cocoa powder

1 teaspoon vanilla extract

Pinch of salt

GANACHE LAYER

1 cup unsweetened chocolate chips

1 cup plant milk

½ cup date sugar

Notes

Store these brownies in the fridge for up to 5 days or in the freezer for up to 2 weeks.

To create a double boiler, pour 2 cups of water into a small pot. Place a glass bowl or stainless-steel pot on top. Set the burner to medium-low heat.

You can also microwave the chocolate to melt it.

I find that running a knife under hot water before cutting the brownies helps to make nice clean edges.

Directions

① Line an 8 x 8-inch square pan with parchment paper and set aside.

② Place the ingredients for the brownie base into a food processor. Process until the mixture comes together to form a thick doughy consistency. The mixture should hold together when you squeeze some in your hand.

③ Press the brownie base into the lined pan until it is compact and even.

④ To melt the chocolate, place the chocolate in the bowl of the double boiler and stir while it melts. Continue to stir the chocolate until it is completely melted and smooth. Turn off the burner. Handle the bowl with care: It will be hot!

⑤ Next, add the plant milk and date sugar to the melted chocolate. Mix well with a whisk until it is nice and smooth.

⑥ Pour the chocolate ganache over the brownie base. Tap the pan to get the top nice and even.

⑦ Place the pan in the fridge for 1 hour, or until the ganache has fully set and cooled.

⑧ Use the parchment paper to remove the brownie base from the pan.

⑨ Cut into squares and serve.

Chocolate-Frosted Carob Donuts

Carob powder is a nutritious, caffeine-free alternative to cocoa, making it a great choice for these cake-style donuts. With their rich, chocolatey flavor, they're perfect for satisfying any donut craving. Keep in mind that carob has a unique taste that's slightly different from chocolate, so feel free to swap in cocoa powder if you'd prefer a classic double-chocolate twist.

DIFFICULTY
Easy

MAKES
4 donuts

Ingredients

DONUTS

1 cup chopped Medjool dates, pitted, or 10 to 12 dates

¼ cup runny tahini

1 teaspoon vanilla extract

½ cup plant milk

¼ cup carob powder

½ cup oat flour

¼ cup almond flour

¾ teaspoon baking powder

¼ teaspoon salt or to taste

FROSTING

6 Medjool dates, pitted

¼ cup hot water

1 tablespoon cocoa powder

1 teaspoon tahini

⅛ cup plant milk or to taste

⅛ teaspoon salt

Directions

1. Preheat the oven to 350°F.
2. Combine the dates, tahini, vanilla extract, and plant milk in a high-speed blender or processor and blend until completely smooth. Add the carob powder and process again until smooth, scraping down the sides as necessary.
3. In a large bowl, combine the oat flour, almond flour, baking powder, and salt.
4. Add the wet ingredients to the dry ingredients. Mix to combine. The batter will be thick.
5. Place the batter in a donut pan and bake for 20 to 25 minutes.
6. Remove the donuts from the oven and allow to cool in the pan for 10 minutes before transferring to a cooling rack.
7. Prepare the frosting by combining all the ingredients in a high-speed blender and blend until smooth.
8. Dip the cooled donuts halfway into the frosting.

Note

Take these donuts up a notch by topping them with crushed nuts or freeze-dried fruit.

HV Carrot Cake

I wanted to create a carrot cake that would pack in all the flavor of a traditional carrot cake but without the unhealthy ingredients, so I'm using my favorite combination of oat and almond flour to replace wheat flour, and instead of refined sugar, I use applesauce and date syrup. To top it all off, I'm adding a rich and creamy vegan cream cheese frosting made from cashews.

DIFFICULTY
Medium

MAKES
9-inch cake

Ingredients

WET

1 cup applesauce
2/3 cup date syrup
1/4 cup plant milk
1 tablespoon apple cider vinegar
1½ teaspoons vanilla
1½ cups grated carrots

DRY

2¼ cups oat flour
1½ cups almond flour
2 teaspoons baking powder
½ teaspoon baking soda
1½ teaspoons ground cinnamon
¼ teaspoon ginger powder
⅛ teaspoon ground cloves
¼ teaspoon ground nutmeg
¼ teaspoon salt

CREAM CHEESE FROSTING

1½ cups raw cashews, soaked for at least 2 hours
½ cup coconut milk or cream (see notes)
2 tablespoons lemon juice
6 Medjool dates, pitted
1 teaspoon vanilla extract

Directions

1. Preheat the oven to 350°F. Line a 9-inch cake pan with parchment paper.
2. In a bowl, place the wet ingredients and mix to combine.
3. In a separate bowl, place all the dry ingredients and whisk together.
4. Pour the wet ingredients into the dry ingredients and mix to combine. Do not overmix.
5. Pour the batter into the prepared cake pan.
6. Bake for 30 to 35 minutes, or until a toothpick inserted in the center comes out clean.
7. Allow to cool for 15 minutes in the cake pan and then transfer to a cooling rack to cool completely.
8. While the cake cools, make the frosting. Drain the cashews and discard the soaking water.
9. Combine the cashews and all the frosting ingredients in a high-speed blender and blend until smooth.
10. Once the cake has cooled completely, spread the frosting onto the cake.

Notes

This cake will keep in the fridge for up to 5 days.

If you are avoiding coconut milk, you can replace it with your plant milk of choice.

Lemon-Blueberry Cake

This is, without a doubt, my favorite cake in this entire book! The vibrant, tangy flavor of the soft lemon cake perfectly complements the natural sweetness of plump, juicy blueberries. Not only is this cake a feast for the taste buds, but it also has some added wholesomeness thanks to the lemon and blueberries. Trust me—one bite, and you'll see why this is such a standout.

DIFFICULTY
Easy

MAKES
one 9-inch cake

Ingredients

DRY

2 cups almond flour

1¼ cups oat flour

2 teaspoons baking powder

1 teaspoon baking soda

½ teaspoon ground turmeric

1 tablespoon lemon zest

1 pint (1¾ cups) fresh blueberries

WET

1 cup chopped Medjool dates, pitted, or 10 to 12 dates

1 cup plant milk

½ cup lemon juice

1½ teaspoons vanilla extract

BLUEBERRY SAUCE

10 ounces (1¼ cups) frozen blueberries, thawed

3 Medjool dates, pitted

2 teaspoons vanilla extract

½ cup toasted dried coconut flakes, for garnish (optional; see note)

Note

Toast some unsweetened dried coconut flakes and sprinkle over the cake as a finishing touch.

Directions

① Preheat the oven to 350°F. Line a 9-inch cake pan with parchment paper and set aside.

② Place all the dry ingredients, except for the blueberries, in a large bowl and mix to combine.

③ In a high-speed blender, combine the dates, plant milk, lemon juice, and vanilla extract and blend until smooth.

④ Add the wet ingredients to the dry ingredients. Mix to combine. Fold in the pint of blueberries to combine.

⑤ Pour the batter into the parchment-lined pan.

⑥ Bake for 20 minutes, then reduce the oven temperature to 325°F.

⑦ Continue to bake for an additional 15 minutes, or until the edges are browned and the top is firm when pressed gently. Allow the cake to cool in the pan until warm (for about 20 minutes).

⑧ While the cake cools, prepare the blueberry sauce. Combine all the ingredients in a medium saucepan on medium-low heat. Bring to a simmer for 10 to 15 minutes. Then turn off the heat and allow to cool. Blend in a high-speed blender until smooth; add water to adjust consistency.

⑨ Pour the blueberry sauce over the top of the cake or add as it's being served. Sprinkle with the coconut flakes, if desired.

Double-Chocolate Banana Bread

Why make banana bread when you can make chocolate banana bread? And why make chocolate banana bread when you can make double-chocolate banana bread? This bread is so rich, moist, and chocolatey that no one would ever guess it's made without oil, wheat, or refined sugar. It is quick and easy, so go ahead and double the batch to keep an extra one on hand!

DIFFICULTY
Easy

MAKES
one 8.5 x 4.5-inch loaf pan

Ingredients

DRY

1½ cups almond flour
½ cup oat flour
5 tablespoons cocoa powder
¼ teaspoon salt
½ teaspoon baking soda
2 teaspoons baking powder
¾ cup date-sweetened chocolate chips, divided

WET

1 cup mashed banana (2–3 ripe bananas)
⅓ cup date syrup
2 teaspoons vanilla extract
1 tablespoon apple cider vinegar

Note

This bread is best enjoyed fresh but can be stored in the refrigerator for up to 3 days.

Directions

① Preheat the oven to 350°F. Line a standard 8.5 x 4.5-inch loaf pan with parchment paper and set aside.

② In a large bowl, place all the dry ingredients except for the chocolate chips and mix to combine.

③ In another large bowl, place all the wet ingredients and mix to combine.

④ Add the wet ingredients to the dry ingredients. Mix until just combined. Fold in ½ cup of the chocolate chips.

⑤ Pour the batter in the lined loaf pan. Top with the remaining ¼ cup chocolate chips.

⑥ Bake for 25 to 30 minutes, or until a toothpick inserted in the middle comes out clean.

⑦ Allow the bread to cool for 10 minutes before transferring to a cooling rack and cutting.

Pecan Pie

Pecan pie was a staple at my childhood family gatherings. Unfortunately, it was often packed with refined sugar, eggs, and butter, making the pie a less-than-healthy indulgence. In this reimagined version, I've swapped out the traditional ingredients for whole dates and date syrup to create that rich, caramel-like pecan filling we all love. Paired with a simple almond flour piecrust, this recipe brings a healthier twist to a holiday favorite. While still quite sweet, this version is lighter, nutrient rich, and a more mindful choice for anyone craving a traditional pecan pie.

DIFFICULTY
Medium

MAKES
one
9-inch pie

Ingredients

CRUST

2 tablespoons ground flaxseed plus 5 tablespoons water (flax egg)

1¼ cups almond flour

⅓ cup arrowroot powder

¼ teaspoon baking powder

¼ teaspoon salt or to taste

FILLING

2 cups pecans, divided

10 Medjool dates, pitted

¾ cup date syrup

3 tablespoons ground flaxseed

1½ teaspoons vanilla extract

¼ teaspoon salt

¼ cup water

Note

Pie will keep in the fridge for up to 1 week or for 1 month in the freezer.

Directions

1. Combine the ground flaxseed and water and set aside.
2. In a large bowl, combine the almond flour, arrowroot powder, baking powder, and salt.
3. Add the flax egg to the dry ingredients and mix with a spoon until it begins to come together and then use your hands to form a ball of dough.
4. Place the ball between two sheets of parchment paper and roll to fit a 9-inch pie pan.
5. Transfer the rolled dough to the pie pan by flipping the bottom parchment paper onto the pan with the rolled dough facing down. Gently use your fingers to press the dough to line the pan. Trim any excess pie dough from around the edges of the pan.
6. Poke the crust with a fork, cover, and place in the freezer for 20 minutes.
7. Preheat the oven to 400°F.
8. Cover the piecrust with parchment and use pie weights or other heat-safe material to weigh the crust down. Bake for

(recipe continues)

Pecan Pie (continued)

15 minutes. Remove from the oven to cool and reduce the oven temperature to 375°F.

9. In a food processor, combine 1 cup of the pecans, dates, date syrup, ground flaxseed, vanilla extract, salt, and water and blend until smooth.

10. To the bottom of the parbaked pie shell, add ½ cup of the pecans. Add the pie filling. Top the pie with the remaining ½ cup of pecans.

11. Bake for 20 minutes, or until the pie is not wet or soft to the touch. Allow to cool and set.

Apple Crumb Pie

There's nothing quite like a classic apple pie. It holds a special place as one of my favorite desserts, so for this recipe I've chosen my favorite apple, Granny Smith. Its subtle tartness balances the sweetness beautifully. While these apples take a little longer to cook, the added tang they bring is well worth the wait, giving this pie its distinctive flavor.

DIFFICULTY
Easy

MAKES
one
9-inch pie

Ingredients

CRUST

2 tablespoons ground flaxseed plus 5 tablespoons water (flax egg)

1¼ cups almond flour

⅓ cup arrowroot powder

¼ teaspoon baking powder

¼ teaspoon salt or to taste

FILLING

4–5 Granny Smith apples

¼ cup date paste (page 43)

1 teaspoon ground cinnamon

1 tablespoon arrowroot powder

2 tablespoons water

TOPPING

½ cup walnuts

½ cup pecans

2 Medjool dates, pitted

½ teaspoon vanilla extract

Note

Pie will keep in the fridge for up to 5 days.

Directions

1. Combine the ground flaxseed and water and set aside.
2. In a large bowl, combine the almond flour, arrowroot powder, baking powder, and salt.
3. Add the flax egg to the dry ingredients and mix with a spoon until it begins to come together, then use your hands to form a ball of dough.
4. Place the ball between two sheets of parchment paper and roll to fit a 9-inch pie pan.
5. Transfer the rolled dough to the pie pan by flipping the bottom parchment paper onto the pan with the rolled dough facing down. Gently use your fingers to press the dough to line the pan. Trim any excess pie dough from around the edges of the pan.
6. Poke the crust with a fork, cover, and place in the freezer for 20 minutes.
7. Preheat the oven to 400°F.
8. Cover the piecrust with parchment and use pie weights or other heat-safe material to weigh the crust down. Bake for 15 minutes. Remove from the oven to cool and reduce the oven temperature to 375°F.

(recipe continues)

Apple Crumb Pie (continued)

9. Peel and cut the apples into slices ¼ inch thick.

10. Place the apples, date paste, cinnamon, arrowroot powder, and water in a large bowl and mix to combine so that the apples are well coated.

11. Pour the filling in the piecrust. Cover with an oven-safe lid or foil.

12. Bake covered for 20 to 25 minutes.

13. Uncover and bake for an additional 5 to 10 minutes, or until the crust is golden brown. Remove from the oven. Let cool for 10 minutes while you prepare the topping.

14. Put the topping ingredients in a food processor and process to a coarse crumb. Top the pie with nut crumbs.

Chocolate Pie with Peanut Crust

When I think of this pie, a few words immediately come to mind: rich, indulgent, and chocolatey! Its creamy, mousse-like filling pairs perfectly with the peanuty, graham-inspired crust, creating a dessert that's nothing short of heavenly. If you have a peanut allergy, don't worry—walnuts or almonds will work beautifully as well.

DIFFICULTY
Easy

MAKES
one
9-inch pie

Ingredients

CRUST

2½ cups peanuts (see notes)

4 Medjool dates, pitted

1 teaspoon vanilla extract

FILLING

12–14 large Medjool dates, pitted

3 cups plant milk

12 ounces unsweetened chocolate (see notes)

Directions

1. Combine the peanuts, dates, and vanilla extract in a food processor. Process to a semi-fine meal. The meal should hold together when squeezed in your hand.
2. Press the crust mix into a 9-inch-wide deep-dish pie pan. Set aside.
3. Blend the dates and plant milk until completely smooth.
4. To melt the chocolate, create a double boiler: Pour 2 cups of water in a small pot. Place a glass bowl or stainless-steel pot on top. Set the burner to medium-low heat. Place the chocolate in the bowl and stir while it melts. Continue to stir the chocolate until it is completely melted and smooth. Turn off the burner. Take care to handle the bowl with care: It will be hot! (You can also microwave the chocolate to melt it.)
5. Add the melted chocolate to the date mixture and blend to combine.
6. Pour the chocolate filling into the piecrust.
7. Refrigerate for a minimum of 4 hours to set the filling.

Notes

NUT-FREE: Use your favorite seed(s) to replace the peanuts in the crust.

This pie will keep in the fridge for up to 5 days.

If you don't want to use peanuts, you can use walnuts or almonds.

You can use chocolate chips or a minced chocolate bar.

Orange Cheesecake Cups

If you love the classic childhood creamsicle flavor, you are going to love this simple cheesecake. A combination of sweet, zesty orange with warm vanilla, it's quick to make and gives you a burst of summer, anytime of the year.

DIFFICULTY
Easy

MAKES
4 servings

Ingredients

CRUST

1 cup raw walnuts or other nut of choice

2 Medjool dates, pitted

½ teaspoon vanilla extract

FILLING

1⅓ cups raw cashews, soaked for at least 2 hours

3 Medjool dates, pitted

1½ teaspoons vanilla extract

½ cup fresh orange juice

2 teaspoons orange zest

Orange slices, for garnish (optional)

Directions

1. Combine the crust ingredients in a food processor and process to a semi-coarse crumb.
2. Lightly press the crust into 4 small glass cups or bowls.
3. Drain the cashews and discard the soaking water. Combine the cashews and other filling ingredients in a high-speed blender and blend until smooth.
4. Pour the filling over the crust and smooth with a spatula. Freeze for 1 to 2 hours, or until firm.
5. Garnish with orange slices, if using.

Note

These will keep in the fridge for up to 5 days or in the freezer for up to 1 month.

NUT-FREE: Use sunflower seeds to replace the cashews in the filling (see page 22) and your favorite seed(s) to replace the nuts in the crust.

Notes

Store in the fridge for up to 5 days or in the freezer for up to 1 month.

Wild blueberries are my favorite because they have a higher concentration of antioxidants and micronutrients.

If you would like to use another kind of fruit, a one-to-one swap will work. You'll want to chop larger fruits into smaller pieces before using.

NUT-FREE: Use sunflower seeds to replace the cashews in the filling (see page 22) and your favorite seed(s) to replace the nuts in the crust.

Blueberry Cheesecake Cups

Cheesecake is one of those desserts that pairs well with fruit. I top these individual-serving cheesecakes with blueberries, but you can use cherries, raspberries, strawberries—or a mix. Not only is the topping flexible, but you can also use your nut of choice for the base. These cups are easy to make and, of course, full of healthy ingredients, so you can indulge freely in this treat!

DIFFICULTY
Easy

MAKES
6 servings

Ingredients

CRUST

1 cup nuts of choice (I like walnuts)

2 Medjool dates, pitted

½ teaspoon vanilla extract

Pinch of salt

FILLING

1½ cups raw cashews, soaked minimum 2 hours

8 Medjool dates, pitted

1 tablespoon lemon juice

1½ teaspoons vanilla

½ cup plant milk

Pinch of salt

TOPPING

15 ounces frozen blueberries, divided (see notes)

Small amounts of water as needed

Directions

1. Combine the crust ingredients in a food processor and blend until the mixture gets sticky. Do not overblend.
2. Divide the crust mixture evenly into 6 muffin molds. Press the mixture to compact at the bottom.
3. Drain the cashews and discard the soaking water. Combine the cashews and other filling ingredients in a high-speed blender and blend until a thick and smooth consistency is achieved.
4. Place an equal amount of filling over the crusts in the muffin molds. Make sure to leave space for the blueberries.
5. Top each cupcake with a spoonful of blueberries (about 5 ounces of blueberries for the 6 cupcakes). Gently press them into the filling center.
6. Freeze for 2 to 3 hours.
7. Before serving, blend the remaining 10 ounces of blueberries for the topping into a smooth, pourable consistency.
8. Remove the cheesecake cups from the freezer. Allow to thaw for a few minutes before removing from the pan. Thaw further depending on the desired consistency.
9. Serve with the blueberry sauce.

Key Lime Cheesecake

This creamy cheesecake is bursting with a fresh, tart flavor from the key lime juice and zest. The rich texture comes from blended cashews while agar agar helps it set perfectly. Instead of a traditional crust, this version uses a naturally sweet and nutty base made from walnuts and dates. It's a delicious, healthier twist on a classic dessert.

DIFFICULTY
Easy

MAKES
one 7-inch springform pan

Ingredients

Crust

1½ cups walnuts

4 Medjool dates, pitted

½ teaspoon vanilla extract

Filling

2 cups cashews, soaked overnight, drained

1½ cups plant milk

11 Medjool dates, pitted (adjust sweetness)

1½ teaspoons vanilla extract

5 tablespoons key lime juice (see notes)

1½ tablespoons key lime zest

¼ cup water

1 teaspoon agar agar powder (see notes)

Directions

1. Place the crust ingredients in a food processor. Pulse into a semi-coarse crumb. Press into the base of a 7-inch springform pan.
2. Place the cashews, plant milk, dates, vanilla extract, lime juice, and lime zest in a high-speed blender and blend until completely smooth.
3. In a small pot, pour the water and agar agar powder and whisk. On medium heat, continue to whisk as the mixture thickens, for about 2 minutes. Remove from the heat.
4. Quickly add the agar agar mixture to the blender with the filling and blend until completely incorporated.
5. Pour the filling into the pan. Allow it to set in the fridge for a minimum of 2 hours.

Notes

This will store in the fridge for up to 5 days.

If you can't find key limes in your area, regular limes will work.

It is important to use agar agar powder and not flakes. If you use agar agar flakes, the cake will not set completely.

This pie can also be prepared in a standard pie pan. You'll want to press the crust firmly up the sides of the pan before pouring in the filling.

NUT-FREE: Use sunflower seeds to replace the cashews in the filling (see page 22) and your favorite seed(s) to replace the nuts in the crust.

Notes

This cheesecake will keep in the fridge for up to 5 days.

You can use fresh or frozen mangoes to make the purée.

It is important to use agar agar powder and not flakes. If you use agar agar flakes, the filling will not set completely.

Using the lesser amount of agar agar in the mango topping will result in a jam-like consistency. Using the larger amount will result in a gelatin-like consistency.

NUT-FREE: Use sunflower seeds to replace the cashews in the filling (see page 22) and your favorite seed(s) to replace the nuts in the crust.

Mango-Chocolate Cheesecake

Mango and chocolate might not be the most obvious pairing, but don't let that stop you. This creamy cheesecake proves just how perfect they can be together. The subtle chocolate flavor from the crust complements the creamy mango filling while a layer of pure mango on top adds a burst of flavor.

DIFFICULTY
Easy

MAKES
one 7-inch springform pan

Ingredients

CRUST

1½ cups walnuts

5 Medjool dates, pitted

½ teaspoon vanilla extract

2 tablespoons cocoa powder

FILLING

1½ cups cashews, soaked overnight, drained

1½ cups mango purée (see notes)

4 Medjool dates, pitted

1½ teaspoons vanilla extract

2 tablespoons lemon juice

¼ cup water

1 teaspoon agar agar powder (see notes)

TOPPING

1 cup mango purée

⅛–¼ teaspoon agar agar powder (see notes)

Directions

1. Place the crust ingredients in a food processor. Pulse into a semi-coarse crumb. Press into the base of a 7-inch springform pan.

2. Place the drained cashews, mango purée, dates, vanilla extract, and lemon juice in a high-speed blender and blend until completely smooth.

3. In a small pot, pour the water and agar agar powder and whisk. On medium heat, continue to whisk as the mixture thickens, for about 3 minutes. When the mixture is thick, remove from the heat.

4. Quickly add the agar agar mixture to the blender with the filling and blend until completely incorporated.

5. Pour the filling into the pan. Allow it to set in the fridge for a minimum of 2 hours.

6. Prepare the mango topping by whisking together the mango purée and agar agar in a small pot. Over medium heat, allow the mixture to come to a gentle boil, for 2 to 3 minutes, stirring constantly. Once the mixture boils and thickens, remove from the heat.

7. Pour the mango topping over the base. Tap the pan to create a smooth top.

8. Set in the fridge for a minimum of 1 hour.

Better Than Soft-Serve Chocolate Ice Cream

Who says you can't have ice cream for breakfast? With these wholesome ingredients, it's a guilt-free treat! This healthier spin on chocolate soft-serve ice cream is rich and creamy. Prep the mixture the night before, and all you'll need is a high-speed blender to whip up this frozen treat when you're ready.

DIFFICULTY
Easy

MAKES
4 servings

Ingredients

- 3 cups plant milk
- 8–10 Medjool dates, pitted
- ¼ cup raw cashews
- ¼ cup rolled oats
- ½ tablespoon chia seeds
- 1 teaspoon vanilla extract
- 6 tablespoons cocoa powder

Directions

1. Place all the ingredients in a high-speed blender and blend until completely smooth.
2. Pour the mixture into 3 standard silicone ice cube molds. Freeze overnight.
3. Transfer the frozen cubes to a high-speed blender and blend until smooth and creamy.
4. Serve and enjoy immediately.

Cherry Ice Cream

Cherry ice cream was one of my all-time childhood favorites, so creating this healthier version has been such a treat for my grown-up self. The best part? t's packed full of juicy whole cherries, just the way I like it!

DIFFICULTY
Easy

MAKES
4 servings

Ingredients

- 1½ cups plant milk
- 4 cups pitted, frozen cherries, divided
- 6–7 Medjool dates, pitted
- ¼ cup rolled oats
- ½ tablespoon chia seeds
- ½ teaspoon vanilla extract
- ¼ teaspoon almond extract (optional)

Directions

1. Place all the ingredients, using only 3½ cups of the cherries, in a h gh-speed blender and blend until complete y smooth.
2. Pour the mixture into 12 large silicone ice cube molds. Freeze overnight.
3. Transfer the frozen cubes to a high-speed blender and blend ur til smooth and creamy.
4. Mix in the remaining ½ cup of cherries.
5. Serve and enjoy immediately.

Notes

Better Than Soft-Serve Chocolate Ice Cream

Keep the frozen ice cream cubes in an airtight container or resealable bag to have on hand for a quick treat.

NUT-FREE: Replace the cashews with half an avocado.

Cherry Ice Cream

Keep the frozen ice cream cubes in an airtight container or resealable bag to have on hand for a quick treat.

Metric Conversions

The recipes in this book have not been tested with metric measurements, so some variations might occur.

Remember that the weight of dry ingredients varies according to the volume or density factor: 1 cup of flour weighs far less than 1 cup of sugar, and 1 tablespoon doesn't necessarily hold 3 teaspoons.

GENERAL FORMULA FOR METRIC CONVERSION

Ounces to grams—multiply ounces by 28.35	Pounds to grams—multiply pounds by 453.5	Cups to liters—multiply cups by 0.24	Fahrenheit to Celsius—subtract 32 from Fahrenheit temperature, multiply by 5, divide by 9
Grams to ounces—multiply ounces by 0.035	Pounds to kilograms—multiply pounds by 0.45		Celsius to Fahrenheit—multiply Celsius temperature by 9, divide by 5, add 32

VOLUME (LIQUID) MEASUREMENTS

1 teaspoon	=	1/6 fluid ounce	=	5 milliliters
1 tablespoon	=	1/2 fluid ounce	=	15 milliliters
2 tablespoons	=	1 fluid ounce	=	30 milliliters
1/4 cup	=	2 fluid ounces	=	60 milliliters
1/3 cup	=	2 2/3 fluid ounces	=	79 milliliters
1/2 cup	=	4 fluid ounces	=	118 milliliters
1 cup or 1/2 pint	=	8 fluid ounces	=	250 milliliters
2 cups or 1 pint	=	16 fluid ounces	=	500 milliliters
4 cups or 1 quart	=	32 fluid ounces	=	1,000 milliliters
1 gallon	=	4 liters		

VOLUME (DRY) MEASUREMENTS

1/4 teaspoon	=	1 milliliter
1/2 teaspoon	=	2 milliliters
3/4 teaspoon	=	4 milliliters
1 teaspoon	=	5 milliliters
1 tablespoon	=	15 milliliters
1/4 cup	=	59 milliliters
1/3 cup	=	79 milliliters
1/2 cup	=	118 milliliters
2/3 cup	=	158 milliliters
3/4 cup	=	177 milliliters
1 cup	=	225 milliliters
4 cups or 1 quart	=	1 liter
1/2 gallon	=	2 liters
1 gallon	=	4 liters

Acknowledgments

Nutrition and health have been a passion of mine for many years, and I'm incredibly grateful to my HV community on Instagram and YouTube, who have taken the time to engage with and support my efforts in sharing accessible, health-promoting recipes and information. Your encouragement and trust mean so much. You've inspired me to create this healthy vegan cookbook and to keep pursuing this path by continuing to help others improve their health and the health of those they care about. Thank you, sincerely!

This book would not have been possible without the guidance and encouragement of what I am coining the "Make Your Own Team."

Wendy Sherman, I truly couldn't have asked for a better agent. Thank you for believing in the *Make Your Own* concept and for all your help and guidance throughout the process of making this cookbook a reality.

Thank you to **Renée Sedliar,** editor extraordinaire—your patience, guidance, and expertise made the entire book-writing journey feel like a breeze. You helped shape and elevate my vision of *Make Your Own*, and I'm so grateful to have had you by my side throughout this process.

To the whole team at Balance: Nzinga Temu, Cisca Schreefel, Terri Sirma, Toni Tajima, Nyamekye Waliyaya, Scott Trebing, Nan Rittenhouse, Alana Spendley, Nana Twumasi, Kate Mueller, Carrie Wicks, and Lori Lewis. Thank you for investing all your abilities and talents into the creation of this book. It would not be the same without each of your contributions.

To my incredible food photography team: Sam Adler and Sally Haus. You were both a pleasure to work with. Your patience, positivity, and can-do attitudes were exceptional. Thank you for hearing my vision and using your incredible talents to manifest each and every recipe as a work of art. Sally, thank you for your willingness to take on my project while on vacation. The book would not be the same without your creative vision. Sam, thank you for opening your home and allowing me to turn your kitchen into a full-blown production zone. I couldn't have asked for a better team to create and work alongside. This book wouldn't be the same without you both.

A big shout-out to **Venu Gopal** for taking a photo of me that was cover-worthy. Your easygoing, accommodating vibe made the uncomfortable process of getting in front of the camera comfortable, and I am grateful for the shots of me you were able to capture.

Thank you to **Dr. Michael Greger**. Your incredible health videos and books have provided me with so much valuable information, which I have implemented into my diet and cooking approach. You are so giving and selfless, and I appreciate you and your work so much.

Thank you to **Dr. Baxter Montgomery**. You were truly a pioneer in the field of health care. Your implementation of a healthy, plant-based diet as a complementary asset in fighting heart disease was masterful. My conversation with you was one of the greatest highlights of my health journey. You were so kind, knowledgeable, brilliant, and humble, and it was a pleasure to briefly get to know you.

Most of all, thank you to **Dr. Joel Fuhrman**. It is your information and clear, concise presentations that provided the facts and guidance I needed to navigate my health journey successfully. Your nutritarian approach is the foundation of my diet and has been life-changing for me and countless others. You are truly my health hero!

Index

Note: Page references in *italics* indicate photographs.

C

Q

V

W

Z